The Second Amendment

Other titles in *The Constitution:*

The First Amendment
Freedom of Speech, Religion, and the Press
ISBN: 0-89490-897-9

The Second Amendment
The Right to Own Guns
ISBN:0-89490-925-8

The Fourth Amendment
Search and Seizure
ISBN: 0-89490-924-X

The Fifth Amendment
The Right to Remain Silent
ISBN: 0-89490-894-4

The Thirteenth Amendment
Ending Slavery
ISBN: 0-89490-923-1

The Fifteenth Amendment
African-American Men's Right to Vote
ISBN: 0-7660-1033-3

The Eighteenth and Twenty-First Amendments
Alcohol—Prohibition and Repeal
ISBN: 0-89490-926-6

The Nineteenth Amendment
Women's Right to Vote
ISBN: 0-89490-922-3

The Second Amendment

The Right to Own Guns

The Constitution

Freya Ottem Hanson

Enslow Publishers, Inc.

44 Fadem Road   PO Box 38
Box 699   Aldershot
Springfield, NJ 07081   Hants GU12 6BP
USA   UK

To five writer friends—
Eileen, Joan, Louise, Vivian, and Willard

Library of Congress Cataloging-in-Publication Data

Hanson, Freya Ottem, 1949–
    The Second Amendment: the right to own guns / Freya
Ottem Hanson.
        p. cm. — (The Constitution)
    Includes bibliographical references and index.
    Summary: Presents an overview of the Second Amendment
of the United States Constitution and examines the debate
that has surrounded the right to bear arms.
    ISBN 0-89490-925-8
    1. Firearms—Law and legislation—United States—
Juvenile literature. 2. United States. Constitution. 2nd
Amendment—Juvenile literature. [1. Firearms—Law and
legislation. 2. United States. Constitution. 2nd
Amendment.] I. Title II. Series: Constitution (Springfield,
Union County, N.J.)
KF3941.Z9H36   1998
344.73'0533—DC21   97-30805
                                CIP
                                AC

Printed in the United States of America

10 9 8 7 6 5 4 3 2 1

Photo Credits: Courtesy of the Bureau of Alcohol, Tobacco, and
Firearms, Washington, DC, p. 85; Freya Ottem Hanson, pp. 8, 21, 39, 58
(bottom), 73, 93; John Hanson, pp. 42, 45, 58 (top), 89; Library of
Congress, pp. 13, 16, 18, 30, 35, 36; National Archives, pp. 12, 28, 47;
Permission granted by Handgun Control, Inc., p 83; Richard Strauss,
Collection of the Supreme Court of the United States, p. 52.

Cover Photo: Corel Corporation

Contents

Children and Guns—A Lethal Combination

While at home alone in Florida, two boys found a loaded gun in a dresser. One boy killed the other. He pointed the gun at his friend's head and pulled the trigger. Both boys were seven years old.[1]

- A sixteen-year-old girl in Minnesota was killed in a triple murder. Her foster father, who had been drinking, took his .22-caliber revolver and in a rage killed his wife, a neighbor, and the girl.[2]

- Three high school students were killed and five more were wounded when a fourteen-year-old fellow student entered the Paducah, Kentucky, high school and fired twelve rounds from a .22 semiautomatic pistol at a group of students finishing a morning prayer session. The shooter had taken the gun from a neighbor's garage the night before.

According to the National Safety Council, each year in America there are approximately 38,000 firearm deaths.[4] Federal Bureau of Investigation (FBI) statistics from 1994 show that of 22,076 murders, firearms were used in 15,456, or 70 percent, of them. A handgun was used in 83 percent of the murders involving firearms.[5] In 1994 firearms were used in 3,532 youth suicides and in 7,347 youth murders in the United States.[6]

No wonder people ask what can be done to stop the violence. Should there be tougher gun control laws in this country? Should guns be banned altogether? Those who oppose gun control claim that stricter laws will not change the number of people who die each year from gunshots. Their claim is that instead of law-obeying citizens' owning guns, guns will then be in

Most firearm murders in the United States are committed with handguns. To stop criminals from buying guns, Congress passed the Brady Law, in 1993. This law requires a five-day waiting period before purchasing a handgun.

the hands of criminals. This group also says the right to own a gun is guaranteed in the United States Constitution. The part of the Constitution that they are talking about is the Second Amendment. It states: "A well-regulated militia being necessary to the security of a free state, the right of the people to keep and bear arms shall not be infringed."[7]

The words of the Second Amendment have puzzled many people since it was written more than two hundred years ago. Some argue that the Second Amendment gives individual citizens the right to own guns. Others say the Second Amendment gives each state the right to have its own military.

What does the Second Amendment really mean? The United States Supreme Court has decided cases about it. The United States Congress has passed firearm laws. State and city lawmakers have passed gun control laws. Some cities have made the possession of a handgun illegal. Some states allow their citizens to carry a concealed weapon without requiring a permit to do so. What does the Second Amendment have to say about guns? And how does it concern young people? Why did the Founding Fathers include this amendment in the Constitution?

An English History— Freedom and Guns

Most of the early American colonists came here from England. In order to understand these early settlers' views of freedom and guns, let's travel across the Atlantic Ocean to Great Britain.

The Magna Carta

The Magna Carta is a document that was signed in 1215 and marked an important step forward in the development of constitutional government and legal ideas in England. In later centuries, much of the rest of the world followed the English model in creating their own governments.

The Magna Carta guaranteed rights to wealthy land barons. Later, all people, both rich and poor, would enjoy the freedoms expressed in the Magna Carta. Sixty-three provisions in the Magna Carta spelled out liberties that would become part of the governments of other countries around the world. One of those governments was the United States. Some of the rights expressed in the Magna Carta are:

1. Fines in proportion to the offense

2. No self-incrimination

3. Right to a jury trial

4. Right to a speedy trial[1]

The barons selected twenty-five of their own people to govern. This was an example of a representative type of government similar to the one we have in the United States today. The Magna Carta was a first step in creating the right of the people to govern themselves. Although the document did not specifically mention weapons, King John signed the document out of fear of the barons' military strength.

Assize of Arms

Only a few years earlier, in 1181, King Henry II of England had signed the Assize of Arms. It allowed every free man in England to own a weapon. The intent was for the king to have an army ready to fight for him at all times. Those same weapons, however, also gave the people power over an oppressive king. For this reason, the Assize of Arms allowed the king to restrict the number and kinds of weapons each person could own.

Petition of Right

Freedom is not easily won. Even with the Magna Carta, the English people had to continue to challenge their king's abuse of power. In the early 1600s, King Charles I abused his power and used it for his own advantage. His soldiers were housed in private homes, and people were imprisoned without a trial. These offenses were not unlike those George III would impose on the American colonies in the late 1700s and early 1800s.

Sir Edward Coke, the highest-ranking judge in the land, spoke out against King Charles I. The king

In 1215, King John of England reluctantly signed the Magna Carta. The barons' military strength gave the landowners power, and the king was afraid of them.

removed him as judge. Sir Edward Coke did not give up. He ran for a seat in the English Parliament and won the election. Because of his effort, the Petition of Right was passed in 1628. This document reaffirmed some of the earlier freedoms the Magna Carta guaranteed.

Coke knew how precious freedom was. What he did not know was that his brave actions would later inspire Americans like Patrick Henry to speak out against the abuses of another English king, George III.[2] Patrick Henry, a Virginian, is most famous for a speech in which he said, "Give me liberty or give me death."

Agreement of the People

While the American colonies formed, England clashed in civil war. In 1649, army leaders opposed to the throne wrote a constitution that limited the power of government. It became known as the Agreement of the People. Although the agreement expressed many freedoms, no one had the power to enforce it.

Shortly after the agreement was passed, a Protectorate ruled England. In 1653, Oliver Cromwell, a military leader, took over the government of England. He was called Lord Protector, and this time in English history became known as the Protectorate,

"Give me liberty or give me death." These words of Patrick Henry were spoken in 1775 before the Virginia Assembly. Patrick Henry favored "bearing arms" and fighting the king of England. Henry's inspiration came from an Englishman named Sir Edward Coke, who had also spoken out against a tyrannical king.

when no king was in power. Cromwell, known for his strong, disciplined army, governed not only England, but Scotland and Ireland as well. He ruled from 1653 until his death in 1658. By then the people wanted a king again, something the colonies would reject.

Game Act

About a decade after Cromwell's rule, Parliament passed a type of "gun control" law. It was called the Game Act of 1671. The wealthy landowners were allowed to own weapons, but the peasants were not. This restrictive gun law was an effort to reserve the "game" animals and hunting lands for the wealthy.

The law was also a way in which King Charles II, who ruled from 1660 through 1685, seized the weapons of his potential enemies and limited their power. King Charles II also imposed other weapon controls. All gunsmiths were required to report their weekly gun sales. No weapons could be imported into England without a license to do so.[3] The Game Law was one of the first controls on weapons in England.

English Bill of Rights

In 1689, William and Mary of the Netherlands became rulers in England. They were forced to consent to the English Bill of Rights. Some of the freedoms this Bill of Rights guaranteed would influence generations to come. Those freedoms included bans on excessive bail, limits on cruel and unusual punishment, freedom of speech for members of Parliament, and freedom to meet with others.

The English Bill of Rights also addressed the ownership of weapons. Only Protestants were allowed the right to possess arms for their own defense. This was a response to the Catholic King James II, who was Mary's father and had ruled until 1688. James II had attempted to disarm the Protestants while allowing the Catholics to bear arms.[4]

The Bill of Rights limited rulers' military power. They were allowed a standing army only if Parliament approved its existence. Similar language would later become a part of our own Constitution. The first ten amendments to our Constitution would even be called by the same name, the Bill of Rights.

Let us go back across the Atlantic Ocean some thirty-five hundred miles, to Lexington and Concord in Massachusetts. The year is 1775. War has broken out between the American colonies and Great Britain. The colonies were having similar problems with an overbearing king. As you might guess, guns were involved.

Colonial America, Guns, and the Revolutionary War

"Freedom" was the cry of the early immigrants who came to America's shores. In 1607, the first permanent English settlement was established in Jamestown, Virginia. Rights protected in the English Magna Carta and the English Bill of Rights were very important to these colonists.

Early Colonial Life

Guns were a part of early colonial life, and were one of the first purchases a colonist made. Guns were not used for sport. Owning a gun was a necessity. Guns served to protect against attacks by American Indians and to hunt animals for food.

In 1770, Georgia passed a law requiring its citizens to carry guns to church. A man could be searched to make sure he obeyed this law.[1] Even in early colonial days, however, there were controls on the use of firearms. A citizen could not hunt or shoot in the streets of most towns, and it was a crime to use a gun to frighten others.[2]

Guns were part of early Colonial life. For protection, the Pilgrims even carried rifles to church.

In some of the colonies every adult male had to join a militia, a citizen army made up of men who gathered for military training. Militias kept law and order. Each man would bring his own gun and provide his own ammunition. For several days each year, the men would gather to learn firearm and military skills. The militias of those times resembled our present-day National Guard. Many colonial towns did not rely entirely on their citizens to provide guns and ammunition. They kept a stockpile of arms and ammunition. These supplies became very important at the time of the Revolutionary War.[3]

Both sides in the Revolutionary War used muskets. Used before the invention of the rifle, muskets were five- to seven-foot-long firearms worn over the shoulder. They fired lead balls that infantrymen had to slide down the barrel manually. The best known was the

Brown Bess musket. It was about five feet long and weighed ten pounds. The gun was not accurate beyond seventy-five yards, and the loading process was slow. Infantrymen would stand side by side to improve their chances of hitting the enemy. They used twenty-one-inch bayonets fixed on the end of their muskets to charge their enemy and finish the battle.[4]

As tensions between England and the colonies grew, England sent more soldiers to America. Soldiers lived in private homes of the colonists. Many of the colonists resented these unwelcome guests.

On April 19, 1775, the Revolutionary War between the colonies and England began at Lexington and Concord, Massachusetts.

Reasons for the Revolutionary War

The king of England expected the American colonies to pay taxes and be loyal to the crown. To support their wars and internal struggles, the English Parliament imposed heavy taxes on the colonies. These taxes continued for about ten years prior to the Revolutionary War. The colonists complained that they did not consent to those taxes, and were given no representation in Parliament.

Parliament continued to pass taxes on the colonies, one of which was a tax on tea. This tax was especially unpopular among the colonists. As a result, several colonists led a protest during which tea was dumped from British ships into the Boston, Massachusetts, harbor. This event is known as the Boston Tea Party.

Great Britain passed more laws. One of the laws closed Boston Harbor until the destroyed tea was paid for. Another law took away the powers of Massachusetts lawmakers. Another law gave those powers to a governor appointed by the king. Thomas Gage, a British general, became governor.

In September 1774, the First Continental Congress met in Philadelphia, Pennsylvania. The delegates agreed that the colonies would not trade with Great Britain unless these harsh tax laws were repealed. Those in attendance did not want a war. They simply wanted Great Britain to listen to their complaints. Despite the pleas, the king of England refused to repeal the tax laws. Instead, in 1775 British troops were sent to put down the rebellion in Massachusetts.

On April 19, 1775, war broke out between the colonies and Great Britain. British General Thomas Gage planned to take the people's weapons and ammunition stored at Concord and Lexington, Massachusetts. Militiamen came out to fight when the British came near their homes.

Outbreak of War

Governor Thomas Gage in Boston, Massachusetts, received orders to take action against the colonists. He did not want to fight a war. He was married to an American and had lived eighteen years in the colonies. But he took his orders from the king, and had been ordered to take up arms against the colonists. On April 18, 1775, the Redcoats, as the British soldiers were called, marched toward Concord. The next day, war broke out.

These first battles of the Revolutionary War showed the bravery of the American colonists. They also proved that the citizen militias were no match for the British Army. Leaders in Massachusetts asked the Continental Congress to make a unified military effort to defeat the British. In order to do this, an army was needed.

The Continental Congress

Less than a month after the Revolutionary War began, the Second Continental Congress met to organize the Continental Army. George Washington was appointed its Commander in Chief. The Second Continental Congress called for the people to "bear arms" and fight the British. Later, in 1791, the words "bear arms" would appear in the Second Amendment of the Constitution.

In addition to establishing an army, the Continental Congress encouraged each colony to establish representative governments. In creating these governments, several of the states included a Bill of Rights in their system. The right to bear arms was included in some of those early declarations.

Virginia, Pennsylvania, North Carolina, Vermont, and Massachusetts declared that the people should have the right to bear arms for the defense of themselves or the common good.[5] George Mason, a member of the lawmaking body of Virginia, known as the House of Burgesses, wrote the Virginia Declaration of Rights. The Virginia document said, "That a well regulated militia, composed of the body of the people, trained to arms, is the proper, natural, and safe defence of a free state."[6] The Virginia Declaration of Rights later served as a model for the drafters of the Bill of Rights. Just as the Virginia Declaration of Rights included a statement of the right to bear arms, so would our Constitution. That statement would become our Second Amendment.

The Declaration of Independence

After a year of fighting, the colonists were more convinced than ever that they should cut all ties with Great Britain. On July 4, 1776, the Continental Congress approved a Declaration of Independence from England.

John Hancock, president of the Continental Congress, was the first to sign the Declaration of Independence. In all, fifty-six men signed the Declaration of Independence. It reads in part: "The history of the present King of Great Britain is a history of repeated injuries and usurpations, all having in direct object the establishment of an absolute Tyranny over these States."

The colonists listed the following complaints against the king of England:

1. Standing armies kept without the consent of the lawmakers in time of peace.

2. Armed troops quartered among them.

3. Trade cut off with all parts of the world.

4. Taxes imposed without their consent.

5. People denied trial by jury.

6. Seas, coasts, and towns, plundered and destroyed.

The representatives declared, "These United Colonies are, and of Right ought to be Free and Independent States; that they are Absolved from all Allegiance to the British Crown."[7] The United States was born.

The Continuing War Effort—Victory

The war with Great Britain was a difficult one. George Washington struggled with the Continental Army.

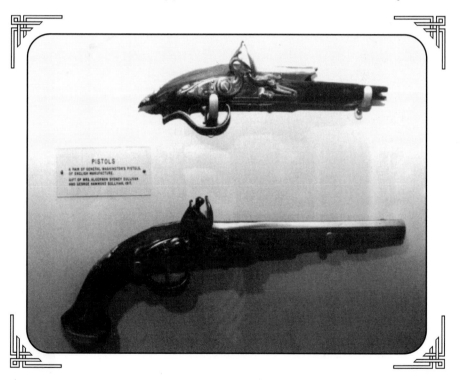

General George Washington's pistols are shown on display at his home at Mount Vernon, Virginia. Most of the Founding Fathers owned firearms. Unlike our weapons of today, these guns were not accurate at long range.

Since all members were volunteers, many soldiers stayed for only a few months and then left. Most were not prepared for a long war, and weapons and supplies were sparse. Without a strong national government, the Continental Congress had to wait for the states to provide money to keep this army going.

The War of Independence continued until 1781, when fighting ended. As the war effort was sustained, additional money was raised. With ammunition, hot meals, and warm clothing, the morale of the soldiers improved. The last major battle of the Revolutionary War was fought in Yorktown, Virginia, in October 1781, before the British surrendered to General George Washington. On September 3, 1783, Congress approved the Treaty of Paris, which granted the United States independence from Great Britain.[8]

The war was over and a great victory had been won. Yet now those original thirteen states faced a bigger struggle. How would they govern themselves? What kind of government would be best? Each of the states had its own government. Many were content to leave it that way. Soon the Founding Fathers discovered that this country would not survive unless changes were made. The Articles of Confederation were inadequate to hold this country together. Something else was needed to create a more perfect union. What would it take? And what would that new government think about guns?

Creating a New Government

The year was 1781. There were no cars or airplanes or trains. There were no telephones, answering machines, fax machines, or Internet services. There was no White House. There was no United States Constitution either. There was no United States of America as we know it today. Instead of fifty states, there were only thirteen. There was a Congress, but it did not have a Senate or House of Representatives. The thirteen states were more like separate countries. Each had its own laws. Although they had united to fight the Revolutionary War, when the war was over in 1781, the states had little reason to work together. Trade squabbles broke out. Each state had its own money. Imagine having to use different money each time you crossed a state line.

The Articles of Confederation

By 1776, the Second Continental Congress had approved a Continental Army and the Declaration of Independence. It also appointed a committee to draw up a plan for a new government for this country. This difficult task resulted in the Articles of Confederation.

The Continental Congress adopted the articles, but it took nearly five years before all thirteen colonies had approved them. The Articles of Confederation governed the United States from 1781 to 1788, when our present Constitution became law. The articles were a first attempt to govern this country, but there were many shortcomings with this government. The states retained their power and little control was handed over to the federal government. The states were suspicious of the powers of a national government.

These same colonists had picked up their guns to fight a war of independence. They did not want to hand over control to a group of people who might be as oppressive as the king of England. Each state wanted its own militia. Each wanted to be able to bear arms and fight against a powerful ruler. The states were not interested in having a national government. If they had one, they were certainly not interested in giving it much power. The national government, under the Articles of Confederation, was limited in these ways:

- All thirteen colonies had to agree on any changes.

- There was no executive branch (president).

- There was no federal court system.

- There was no authority to control the trade between the states.

- There was no taxation of the states unless they consented.

The postwar years were rocky times. States taxed each other, and the debts of the Revolutionary War went unpaid. Because of unstable conditions, Great Britain refused to reopen lines of trade with America.

Rebellions started, and disagreements over waterways and trade between the states continued.

These conditions bothered several of the Founding Fathers. One of them was James Madison of Virginia. He called a meeting in Annapolis, Maryland, to settle trade problems between the states. All of the states were asked to send delegates, but only five states participated. Maryland, the host state, did not even bother to send delegates.

Such lack of interest would have discouraged most people, but two who were present, James Madison and Alexander Hamilton, did not give up. Instead they urged every state to send delegates to another convention scheduled to begin May 14, 1787, in Philadelphia, Pennsylvania.

The future of this new nation was at stake. Who would come to Philadelphia? What would happen there? Would there be changes to the Articles of Confederation? Would a whole new form of government be established? The future of this country depended on what those delegates did.

The Constitutional Convention

Instead of starting May 14, the Constitutional Convention did not begin until May 25. Bad weather delayed the arrival of many delegates. James Madison was the first to arrive in Philadelphia. Twelve states were represented at the convention. Rhode Island refused to come. It did not want any changes made to the Articles of Confederation.

Over the summer months of 1787, the fifty-five delegates met and debated. Some delegates left and never returned to the convention, but most stayed. The Constitution they wrote is the same one we have today. Only twenty-seven amendments have been added to it. The first ten of those amendments, known as the Bill of Rights, were made a part of the Constitution on December 15, 1791.

Independence Hall was the place where the delegates met. Both the Articles of Confederation and the Declaration of Independence were also signed there. The delegates chose George Washington as chairman, and established rules of order. One rule was that each state would have only one vote at the convention. Another rule was that of secrecy. The press was not informed of what was going on. Security guards were posted, eavesdroppers chased away, and delegates warned not to write home about the proceedings.

Once the rules were agreed upon, plans were discussed. The "Virginia Proposal" was presented first. This proposal suggested that population would determine how many representatives a state would have in Congress. The more populated states would have more representatives than the less populated ones. Virginia was the most populous state at that time.

The "New Jersey Proposal" was just the opposite. It suggested that states be given equal representation. A compromise plan was finally approved. There would be two houses of Congress. One, the Senate, would have equal representation from each state. The other, the House of Representatives, would have membership based on population. For example, today California is the most populous state. It has more members in the House of Representatives than any other state. California has only two senators, however, like every other state.

Many different ideas were discussed during that hot summer of 1787. The delegates debated whether to have a president at all. They did not want another king like George III ruling this country. Toward the end of the convention, Benjamin Franklin, the oldest delegate, spoke. He said, "I agree to this Constitution, with all its faults if they are such."[1] As flawed as it was, these delegates could not have realized how well this Constitution would serve the United States in the centuries ahead.

On September 17, 1787, the delegates approved the new Constitution. George Washington was the first to give his approval. His presence and leadership were important to the success of the Constitutional Convention. A total of thirty-nine delegates gave their approval. Thirteen had left or were not present. Only three delegates refused to sign the document. One of them was George Mason. As part of the Constitution, he wanted a Bill of Rights that would guarantee freedoms to the people and to the states. One of those freedoms was the right to "bear arms."

The Delegates

Who were the fifty-five men who came to Philadelphia to create a more perfect union? These men are called our Founding Fathers. Their average age was forty-two. The youngest delegate was twenty-six, and the oldest, Benjamin Franklin, was eighty-one. George Washington was fifty-five. The delegates were also well educated. Many were lawyers, several were farmers, and some were merchants. One was a doctor. Over half of the delegates had a college education. Most of the delegates lived on the East Coast. Most had served in the Revolutionary War, and many held public offices in their home states.

Two delegates are especially important to remember in the drafting of the Constitution and Bill of Rights. One was James Madison. The other was George

James Madison, the fourth president of the United States, is called the "Father of the Constitution." He wrote most of the document. He also introduced the Bill of Rights in Congress and sought its approval. Included in the Bill of Rights is the Second Amendment, which deals with guns.

Mason. James Madison (1751–1836), only thirty-six years of age, was the youngest of the Virginia delegates. He is known as the Father of the Constitution because he wrote most of it. James Madison was a student of different governments. He knew that the Articles of Confederation would not be strong enough to govern this nation. He also knew that a federal government should not be too powerful. The "Virginia Plan," which he wrote, included "checks and balances." Although some of the plan was not adopted, much of it was. This plan guaranteed that none of the three branches of government (executive, legislative, and judicial) could become too powerful. They would have to work together.

Although Madison had been sickly as a child, he lived eighty-five years. He served our country for more than forty of those years. Here are some of his achievements:

• President of the United States (two terms)

• Author of much of the Constitution of the United States

- Author of much of the United States Bill of Rights
- Secretary of State
- Author of the "Federalist Papers"
- Service in the U.S. House of Representatives
- Service at the U.S. Continental Congress
- Member of the Virginia Assembly
- President of the University of Virginia

Madison was willing to change his mind if the common good would be served. One such change of opinion concerned the Bill of Rights. At first, Madison did not think a Bill of Rights was necessary. Later, it was Madison who would propose it and seek its ratification. Unlike George Washington, who was welcomed to Philadelphia in 1787, James Madison arrived almost unnoticed. Yet both made important contributions to our system of government as we know it today.

George Mason (1725–1792) was sixty-two and the oldest of the Virginia delegates who attended the Constitutional Convention. He refused to sign the Constitution. His major objection was the fact that the document had no Bill of Rights. He urged the convention to adopt one and even offered to write it. He said such a protection "would give great quiet to the people."[2] Although his proposal was not accepted at the Constitutional Convention, the Bill of Rights was later adopted. As a result, he became known as the Father of the Bill of Rights.

George Mason also opposed a provision in the Constitution that allowed the importing of slaves. He felt the practice needed to be stopped immediately. Again his ideas were not adopted. Unlike most

George Mason is known as the Father of the Bill of Rights. He was one of three who refused to sign the Constitution. He wanted the Bill of Rights, similar to the one he wrote for his home state of Virginia, to be included. Later Mason's proposal became our United States Bill of Rights on December 15, 1791.

of the delegates, George Mason preferred to stay out of public life. He did, however, have a great influence on the writing of the Bill of Rights. While serving in the House of Burgesses in Virginia, he wrote and introduced the Virginia Declaration of Rights. This document later served as the pattern for our Bill of Rights. Madison used it as a guide when he introduced the Bill of Rights in Congress.

Three Who Did Not Come to Philadelphia

Several famous Americans did not come to the Constitutional Convention. Thomas Jefferson, author of the Declaration of Independence and our third president, was serving as ambassador to France. John Adams, our second president, was in Great Britain. Patrick Henry also did not attend. Although this Virginian was elected as a delegate, he declined. He feared the convention would give too much power to a central government. He had been one of the first to urge his state to arm militias for war against Great Britain.

The Ratification Process

Once the Constitutional Convention was over, a bigger and more difficult task awaited the delegates. Could they convince each state to approve this new government? It would take the approval of nine states. The process was known as ratification.

Alexander Hamilton, James Madison, and John Jay wrote papers in support of the work of the Constitutional Convention. These papers were known as the "Federalist Papers," and were published in many major newspapers. The states were urged to approve the new government.

The new government would have two houses in Congress, a president, and a federal court system. Congress would be given powers it did not have under the Articles of Confederation. It could regulate trade, borrow money, coin money, establish post offices, and declare war. The Congress could raise and support an army and a navy, and call out the state militias to suppress rebellions or invasions.

It took only nine months to ratify the Constitution. On June 21, 1788, New Hampshire became the ninth state to approve the new government. The Constitution was now the law of the land. While there was much to celebrate, many states knew something was missing. That missing link was the Bill of Rights.

The Bill of Rights

Early in the ratification process, several states demanded the Bill of Rights. The delegates to the Constitutional Convention were not opposed to one. Some did not think it was necessary, however. They were convinced that freedoms were already protected in the Constitution itself. Others thought the Bill of

Rights would be too difficult to write. They wondered which freedoms to include and which to exclude. In response to the demands of several states, James Madison proposed twelve amendments to the Constitution. He introduced them in Congress.

The Bill of Rights guaranteed certain rights. One was the right to bear arms. Others were the right to freedom of religion, assembly, the press, and also the right to

- Security in your home from unreasonable searches and seizures.

- A grand jury indictment before being tried in a capital crime (usually murder).

- A jury trial.

- A speedy and public trial.

- An attorney when accused of a crime.

- Reasonable bail.

- No cruel or unusual punishment.

- No housing of soldiers in homes without the owner's consent during times of peace.

- States having powers not granted the federal government.

What about the Second Amendment? What did it say? Why was it included? James Madison's first proposal of the Second Amendment read as follows:

> The right of the people to keep and bear arms shall not be infringed; a well armed, and well regulated militia being the best security of a free country; but no person religiously scrupulous of bearing arms, shall be compelled to render military service in person.[3]

Congress approved the amendment but shortened

it. The clause about religious scruples was deleted. These lawmakers did not want any excuses for avoiding military duty. To this day, however, conscientious objection is a valid reason for not entering military service. The final draft of the Second Amendment was shortened to twenty-seven words. It read as it appears today: "A well regulated Militia, being necessary to the security of a free State, the right of the people to keep and bear Arms, shall not be infringed."[4]

At the time, this particular amendment did not generate much interest. Almost without mention, it was accepted as part of the Bill of Rights. On September 25, 1789, Congress adopted the twelve amendments. By December 15, 1791, the necessary number of states ratified ten of them. Why was the Second Amendment included in the Bill of Rights? What did it mean to the Founding Fathers?

Would they give the Second Amendment a different meaning today from the one they did in 1789? Let's find out what happened to this amendment in the two centuries that followed.

5

The Federal Government and Firearms

For me the pursuit of happiness was shattered by an Intratec TEC-9 assault weapon on a normal sunny business day afternoon in San Francisco. My wife wasn't shot once, she wasn't shot twice . . . she was shot five times."[1] The speaker urged the United States Senate in 1993 to ban assault weapons. A representative of a law enforcement group had a different opinion: "Any proposal to ban a class of rifles and handguns incorrectly labeled 'assault weapons' is not good legislation. It will not protect law enforcement. It will not protect citizens. It will not affect criminal behavior."[2] There have been heated debates in the United States Congress over gun control for a long time. Interest in this subject is not new for lawmakers.

In 1934, the first federal law regulating guns passed the United States Congress. Those who introduced the act in Congress feared that the Supreme Court would rule a gun law unconstitutional. So, the drafters introduced the law as part of a tax bill, allowing the federal government the authority to tax certain sales of firearms. These bills came at a time when public opinion dictated a change in attitude. Criminal activity with the use of such firearms made their regulation imperative. Congress passed laws that affected the whole firearms industry.[3]

Gun Control Laws Passed by Congress

On June 26, 1934, Congress passed the National Firearms Act, and the Bureau of Alcohol, Tobacco, and Firearms (BATF) was established to enforce this law. This law banned certain types of weapons. One was a sawed-off shotgun with a barrel shorter than eighteen inches long. Machine guns, certain rifles, and silencers were also regulated under this law. The law required them to be registered with the BATF, and each firearm had to display an identification number. All manufacturers, importers, and dealers of firearms were required to pay registration fees to the Treasury Department for such weapons and to keep records of those firearms sales.[4]

The United States Supreme Court in the 1939 case of *United States v. Miller* ruled that the 1934 National Firearms Act was constitutional.

In 1938, the Federal Firearms Act was passed. It remained in effect for thirty years. The 1938

A soldier loads ammunition for a machine gun. A federal law in 1934 regulated the use and possession of machine guns, a favorite weapon of gangsters.

The death of civil rights leader Martin Luther King, Jr., led to new firearm laws. The 1968 Gun Control Act limited sales of guns through the mail.

law required those who made or sold firearms, including retail stores, to have a federal license. These federal firearms licensees had to keep records of all gun sales.

This act restricted felons from receiving or shipping a firearm across a state line. It became a federal crime to possess a stolen gun or ammunition. However, a person could purchase a gun through the mail or could go to another state and buy a gun.[5]

Gun Control Becomes More Restrictive

The nation grieved following the assassinations of President John F. Kennedy in 1963, Dr. Martin Luther King, Jr., in 1968, and Senator Robert Kennedy in 1968. As a result, Congress passed the Gun Control Act of 1968. Some parts of this new law were the same as those in the Federal Firearms Act of 1938. For example, those who made guns and those who sold them had to be licensed and had to keep records. Identification numbers on firearms could not be changed, and felons could not have guns.

The law did make certain changes, however. There were more controls on firearms sales than before.

- Handguns could not be sold to out-of-state residents.

- A person had to be twenty-one to purchase a handgun.

- Certain people, such as felons or the mentally ill, could not have guns.

Other limitations were also enacted into law.

- Mail-order firearms and ammunition sales were prohibited except between licensed dealers.

- Records of sales were to be kept and made available for police inspection.

- Buyers of guns had to sign that they were not disqualified from having a gun.

- Firearms and ammunition could be purchased only by those eighteen or older.

- A gun used in violation of this law could be taken away from that person.[6]

Neither pro-gun nor anti-gun groups supported this law. Gun advocates wanted to be able to order guns through the mail. Dealers did not like keeping records of all gun sales. Anti-gun groups thought there should be even more control on the sale of guns.

Rights Regained by Gun Owners

Eighteen years later, a new gun control law was passed. This law gave more rights to gun owners. In 1986, the 99th Congress passed the Firearms Owners' Protection Act. Gun ownership was made more accessible. The sale of weapons to out-of-state residents was allowed, and mail-order purchases of guns again became legal. A person could transport weapons across state lines provided certain conditions were met. Dealers were not required to do as much record-keeping of sales. A gun could not be taken from a person without a court hearing.

The law did place more restrictions in certain areas. The private ownership of a machine gun was banned if the gun was not owned prior to 1986.[7]

Armor-Piercing Ammunition

Most police officers wear bulletproof vests. The vest is worn over the chest and back and is made of material that protects the officer from lead bullets. Most ammunition is made of lead; however, certain bullets made of steel, brass, iron, copper, or bronze are more likely to pierce a bulletproof vest. In 1986, these hard metal bullets, known as cop-killer bullets, were made illegal. A gun dealer who sold such ammunition could have his license revoked.[8]

Plastic Guns Outlawed

Airport and airplane safety continues to be a world-wide concern. In 1988, Congress passed a law that banned the manufacture, import, sale, and possession of plastic firearms. A plastic firearm was defined as one having less than 3.7 ounces of metal. Metal-detecting machines in airports could not identify a plastic gun. The law also said that it was illegal to have a gun that did not look like a gun. For example, a pen or flashlight that was also a gun would be illegal.[9] Toy guns also became suspect. In 1988, a law was passed that said a toy gun must have an orange plug inserted in the barrel. Toy guns had to look obviously different from real weapons. This was the first time the manufacture of toy guns came under the control of Congress.[10] In recent years, many special-interest groups have wondered whether children should play

Two police officers examine a bulletproof vest that could cost five hundred dollars (top). In 1986 Congress passed a law banning armor-piercing ammunition. These "cop-killer bullets" could shoot through protective clothing. A 1988 law of Congress makes it illegal to make or possess a plastic gun. X-ray machines in public buildings and airports are unable to detect firearms not made of metal (bottom).

with toy guns at all. Those opposed to guns have also raised concerns about "super soakers." These large machine-gun-like plastic water guns resemble assault weapons.

More Gun Control in the 1990s

In 1990, Congress passed the Gun-Free School Zones Act. Among other provisions, this law made it illegal to possess a gun within a certain distance of a school.[11] The Supreme Court, however, later held that this law was unconstitutional. Congress did not have the constitutional authority to pass such a law. Although it may seem that the Supreme Court was not concerned about school safety, what the Court decided was that the states, not Congress, must pass these laws. See Chapter 6 for more details on this case.

Brady Act Passed After Years of Waiting

In a 1981 assassination attempt on President Ronald Reagan, Press Secretary James Brady was shot in the head and permanently injured. He and his wife are leaders of a group known as Handgun Control, Inc. In November 1993, after more than a decade of efforts on their part, Congress passed the Brady Handgun Violence Prevention Act. This act regulates the sale of handguns and requires a five-day waiting period between applying for a handgun and buying it. During that time, police officers make background checks on the person applying. If the background check reveals a felony record or other disqualifying factors, the sale will not be permitted. The bill also provided for a system of instant background checks to be up and running in this country by November 30, 1998.

The Brady Act affects all states. If a state already had a more restrictive waiting period than the one in the bill, the Brady Act would not be needed. Initially twenty-nine states and territories needed to comply with the five-day waiting period under the Brady Act.[12]

Those in favor of the bill hoped more people with criminal records would be stopped from purchasing handguns. They also believed a waiting period would be effective as a cooling-off period so that crimes of passion would be reduced. A "crime of passion" is one committed in anger or rage. A "cooling-off period" allows time to calm down.

Brady Act Challenged

On June 27, 1997, the United States Supreme Court ruled that parts of the Brady Act were unconstitutional. Justice Antonin Scalia wrote the 5–4 decision. It held that the United States Congress could not require the chief law-enforcement officer of a state to conduct background checks to see if a person was a felon. In essence, the Court's opinion was that Congress had overstepped its authority. The Court's decision did not invalidate the five-day waiting period. Essentially, however, the background check is optional for state authorities unless state laws require it.

Dissenting Justice John Paul Stevens said, "Article I, Section 8 [of the Constitution] grants the Congress the power to regulate commerce among the states. . . . There can be no question that that provision adequately supports the regulation of commerce in handguns effected by the Brady Act."[13]

Congress's Ban on Assault Weapons

In 1989, Patrick Purdy opened fire on a California elementary schoolyard with an assault rifle. He killed five children, and wounded twenty-nine other children and one teacher. As a result, several states, including California, banned semiautomatic assault weapons. In 1994, a law of Congress did the same.

The Violent Crime Control and Law Enforcement Act of 1994 bans the manufacture and possession of semiautomatic weapons. Certain firearms used in hunting were exempt from the ban, however. A semiautomatic weapon may be a rifle, handgun, or shotgun. Weapons such as the Street Sweeper, the Uzi, the Colt AR-15, and the Intratec TEC-9 were banned.[14]

A semiautomatic weapon can shoot several bullets in rapid succession when the trigger is held down. The gun inserts a new bullet into the chamber automatically. It is a little like a camera that moves your film forward without being wound by hand.

Gun Ban for Those Convicted of Domestic Violence

Domestic violence is an act of physical force or attempted physical force against a family member. Many times domestic violence is between a husband and a wife or a parent and a child. A 1996 federal

law made it illegal for anyone convicted of domestic violence to have a gun or ammunition in his or her possession.[15] As a result of the law, several police officers and hunters who had misdemeanor

Our nation's Capitol building in Washington, D.C., is home to the Senate and the House of Representatives. Federal laws are made here, including laws that regulate guns.

records had to give up their guns. No doubt cases will be filed in federal courts challenging this law.

Presently there are new laws before Congress. One bill asks for a new understanding of what the Second Amendment means. Another is known as Brady II. It would expand gun control measures. All handgun owners would need licenses, and purchases of handguns would be restricted to no more than one per month.

Other proposals include licensing all gun dealers and restricting firearm sales to places of business. In other words, all sales out of a home would be illegal. A proposed law would require gun safety training for all who own guns. Adults would be required to store all guns in a safe place, away from children. Adults who failed to keep guns away from children sixteen or younger could be charged with a crime.[16]

Federal Government Involvement

Since the first federal gun control law was passed in 1934, the federal government has been involved in regulating guns. The federal government takes its authority from both the power to regulate commerce between the states and the power to tax. As long as public opinion demands regulation, members of Congress will have a difficult time ignoring the public outcry for help against acts of violence.

What is the best way to protect the public from violence? Does gun control make a difference? For over sixty years, Congress has passed gun control laws. In doing so, it determined that the Second Amendment does not restrict their right to regulate firearms, including who can own them and who can sell them. Next we will look at what the United States Supreme Court has said about the Second Amendment as it relates to guns and the public.

The Supreme Court and the Second Amendment 6

The United States Constitution establishes three parts of the federal government. They are known as the executive, the legislative, and the judicial branches. The executive branch consists of the president and his cabinet. The legislative consists of the House of Representatives and the Senate. The judicial branch consists of federal courts, of which the highest is the United States Supreme Court.

The Supreme Court's Chief Justice and eight Associate Justices are appointed for life. The Court has the authority to make decisions about the United States Constitution and what it means. It also has the authority to declare a law of Congress unconstitutional.

Since 1803, the Supreme Court has exercised the authority to review laws of Congress and decide whether those laws are constitutional. In that year, Chief Justice John Marshall's famous *Marbury* v. *Madison* decision gave the Court its power of judicial review. This means the Supreme Court has the authority to decide cases about the Bill of Rights, including the Second Amendment. Before we turn to those cases, let's first find out a little more about the work of the United States Supreme Court.

What the Supreme Court Does

The United States Supreme Court Justices decide how certain issues relate to the Constitution. To make these decisions, members of the Court review earlier Court decisions. This process is called "looking at precedent" (what was decided before). The Court may decide to overturn an earlier Court's decision; but, most of the time the Court follows precedent. When a decision is made, it may be unanimous (all nine Justices agree), or there may be a majority opinion (an opinion that a majority of the Justices favor) and a minority opinion (an opinion that the dissenting justices favor).

Sometimes it takes several years for a case to come before the Supreme Court because the Court decides only a limited number of cases each year. The Supreme Court reviews cases that were first decided in a lower court. Those lower courts may be federal district courts, federal appellate courts, or the highest court of a state. Courts in

The Supreme Court building in Washington, D.C., is where the highest court in the land hears cases. The Supreme Court consists of a Chief Justice and eight Associate Justices. Although the Court has decided several gun cases, only four are on the Second Amendment.

two different federal districts or two different states may have made different decisions about the same legal issue. Then the Supreme Court may decide which one should be final. The Supreme Court does not decide every case presented to it. When the Court refuses to hear a case, it "denies *certiorari*." In those cases, the lower court's decision remains as law.

The Supreme Court and the Second Amendment

What has the United States Supreme Court said about the Second Amendment? Since 1791 when this amendment was ratified, only four cases that refer directly to the Second Amendment have been decided. This stands in sharp contrast to other amendments, especially the First Amendment, about which hundreds of cases have been decided.

The first Supreme Court decision on the Second Amendment came one hundred years after the Declaration of Independence was signed. That is a long time for the Court to remain silent. We do not know why the Court was silent on the right to bear arms. When the Court finally did decide a case on the Second Amendment, the case was actually more about civil rights (the rights of citizens) than about guns. This case did, however, establish a precedent about the Second Amendment that has stood for a long time.

United States v. Cruikshank

Shortly after the Civil War ended, William Cruikshank, a white citizen, banded together with others in Louisiana who wanted to deprive blacks of their rights. Cruikshank was charged with thirty-two counts of conspiracy under the federal Enforcement Act of 1870.[1] Cruikshank had disturbed a political

In 1876, Supreme Court Chief Justice Morrison R. Waite wrote the decision in the first case about the Second Amendment. United States v. Cruikshank *said that the Second Amendment did not protect the right to "bear arms" from local interference. Instead the amendment had no other effect than to restrict the powers of the national government.*

meeting in which African Americans were gathering. He deprived them of their guns and prevented them from assembling. Cruikshank appealed. He claimed his crimes were not federal crimes against the United States. The Supreme Court agreed in a unanimous decision.[2]

Chief Justice Morrison R. Waite wrote the majority decision for the Court in 1875. The Court held that the federal crime charges were inappropriate because they did not involve the denial of the victims' federal rights. The constitutional rights to assemble and to bear arms protected citizens only from congressional interference. They did not protect from interference from private citizens. The next Supreme Court decision, *Presser v. Illinois,* was decided a decade later, in 1886.

Presser v. Illinois

In 1879, Herman Presser was indicted in criminal court, Cook County, Chicago, Illinois. He was found guilty of violating an Illinois military law that required parade participants to obtain a permit in order to carry a gun. Presser had founded a military organization in which the members studied laws and performed military drills. Although the group did not have a license to march, which the law required, Presser rode on a horse as some four hundred of his armed men participated in a parade.[3]

Presser was sentenced to pay a fine of ten dollars. Presser appealed to the United States Supreme Court. He claimed his Second Amendment right to "bear arms" had been violated. The Court did not agree with Presser.

Justice William B. Woods wrote the opinion for a unanimous Court. The opinion stated that Presser's Second Amendment rights had not been infringed upon. The Second Amendment limited the federal government, not state governments, from passing firearm laws. The Supreme Court declared the Illinois law constitutional. What can we learn about the meaning of the Second Amendment from this decision? We can conclude that the Supreme Court judged the Second Amendment not to guarantee individuals the absolute right to have firearms.

Miller v. Texas

Eight years after the *Presser* case, the *Miller* v. *Texas* case regarding the Second Amendment was heard. Franklin P. Miller, a Texan, carried a pistol on the public streets of a Texas town in violation of state law. He shot and killed a man, and was sentenced to death. Miller appealed. He said the Texas law violated his Second Amendment right to "bear arms."[4]

The Supreme Court did not agree with Miller. The decision said the Texas law did not violate Miller's Second Amendment rights. States had the power to enact their own firearm laws. This decision of the Supreme Court was similar to the previous two others on the Second Amendment. Justice Henry B. Brown wrote the Court's opinion. It said, "It is well settled that the restrictions of these amendments operate only upon the Federal power, and have no reference whatever to proceedings in state courts."[5] For the third time, the Supreme Court said that the Second Amendment did not protect an individual's right to a firearm.

United States v. Miller

For the next forty-five years, the Supreme Court remained silent about the Second Amendment. With the passage of federal firearm legislation in the mid-1930s, the Court was again challenged to decide what the Second Amendment was all about. Could the federal government make laws concerning guns? The case of *United States* v. *Miller* was decided in 1939.[6]

Jack Miller and Frank Layton were found guilty of taking an unregistered sawed-off shotgun across state lines. They carried a double-barrel, twelve-gauge Stevens shotgun in their car from Claremore, Oklahoma, to Siloam Springs, Arkansas. The 1934 National Firearms Act made it illegal to possess a gun with a barrel shorter than eighteen inches long unless it was registered. Their acts broke this federal law. The defendants claimed their Second Amendment rights were violated. The case was appealed from an Arkansas court to the Supreme Court.

Justice James C. McReynolds wrote the Court's opinion. The Supreme Court held that the National Firearms Act of 1934 did not violate the defendants' Second Amendment rights under the Constitution. The Court wrote that a shotgun having a barrel shorter than eighteen inches long had no reasonable relationship to a well-regulated militia. The Second

Amendment, thus, did not guarantee a right to possess such a weapon.

A federal gun law was upheld as constitutional for the first time. This is the last time the Court wrote an opinion directly relating to the Second Amendment. The Court has not, however, remained silent about gun control. Two major cases have come before the Supreme Court in the 1990s.

United States v. Lopez

In 1990, Congress passed a law making it illegal to have a gun within a thousand feet of a public school. Those who favored the law argued that because Congress has the authority under the United States Constitution to regulate commerce, it also has the right to regulate the possession of firearms near a public school.[7] Two federal courts issued decisions about the Gun-Free School Zones Act of 1990. Their decisions were different. The Ninth Circuit Court of Appeals found the law was constitutional. The Fifth Circuit Court of Appeals found it was not.

In passing gun control laws, Congress originally claimed its authority under the commerce clause and the taxation clause of the United States Constitution. In doing so, Congress claimed a "dual sovereignty" to regulate firearms. This meant that both the federal and state governments could pass laws about guns.

The argument was that because firearms are often transported across state lines, Congress could regulate their use and possession around a public school. The Supreme Court said no and declared the law unconstitutional.

In 1995, the Supreme Court decided to review the case of *United States* v. *Lopez*. Alfonso Lopez, Jr., entered Edison High School in San Antonio, Texas.

He was hired to deliver a .38-caliber handgun to a student there. Although the gun was not loaded, Lopez did have bullets in his possession. He was charged with violation of the Gun-Free School Zones Act. He pleaded not guilty.

Lopez claimed that the Gun-Free School Zones Act was unconstitutional. The Fifth Circuit Court of Appeals agreed with Lopez. It wrote that "management of education is a state responsibility, and not one for the federal government." The Ninth Circuit Court of Appeals held in a different case that the Gun-Free School Zones Act was constitutional. The Supreme Court had the final say.

On April 26, 1995, the Supreme Court announced its decision. The Court ruled the 1990 law of Congress unconstitutional. Majority and minority opinions were filed. Chief Justice William H. Rehnquist wrote the majority opinion. It held that the powers of Congress did not cover this law, and that there should not be federal involvement. These matters were of local concern. What the majority opinion said was that each state, not Congress, should pass laws concerning schools.

Justice Stephen Breyer wrote a minority opinion. This opinion said Congress should have the right to pass laws where the social well-being of Americans is affected. The minority believed that schools were one of those areas of concern.[8]

What does this decision of the Supreme Court mean? The majority opinion did not say that guns should be allowed around schools. What it did say was that Congress should not make those laws; rather, local and state governments were in charge of regulating the schools. What do you think?

The Supreme Court has the power to decide whether or not gun-control laws of Congress are constitutional. The current members of the Supreme Court are as follows: Back row, left to right: Ruth Bader Ginsburg, David Souter, Clarence Thomas, Byron White. Front row, left to right: Antonin Scalia, John Stevens, Chief Justice William Rehnquist, Sandra Day O'Connor, and Anthony Kennedy.

Printz v. United States

The United States Supreme Court heard legal arguments in the case *Printz* v. *United States* in December 1996.[9] It is known as the constitutional challenge to the Brady Act. The case was heard under the Tenth Amendment, which states that authority not specifically given to the federal government is reserved to the states.

The opponents of the Brady Act claimed that Congress could not require state or local law-enforcement officers to do background checks on purchasers of handguns. The United States Supreme Court's decision supported Jay Printz, a sheriff and coroner in Ravalli County, Montana. The part of the Brady Act that required officers to do background checks was found unconstitutional. The five-day waiting period, however, was not challenged and remains law.

Those on the Supreme Court who supported the Brady Act wrote a dissenting opinion. The opinion quoted a February 1997 United States Department of Justice report: "Between 1994 and 1996 approximately 6,600 firearm sales each month to potentially dangerous persons were prevented by Brady Act checks; over 70 percent of the rejected purchasers were convicted or indicted felons."[10] The dissenting Justices believed that Congress had authority to respond to an epidemic of gun violence.

The Supreme Court has decided only four cases that relate directly to the Second Amendment. That is not very many cases. Other firearm laws have been challenged under other parts of the Constitution, however. More than two hundred years have passed since the Second Amendment became law. In the Second Amendment cases presented, the Court has held that the Second Amendment is not about the absolute right of an individual to have a gun. Both state and federal governments have the power to pass certain laws restricting the possession and use of guns. Such laws do not violate the Second Amendment. Now let's find out how the states have handled the right to bear arms.

The States and Guns

There are over twenty thousand gun control laws in this country. Most are state and local laws. The laws of one state may differ greatly from those of a bordering state. And in some states, the laws vary from city to city. Let's look at state constitutions first.

Constitutions of the States

The United States has a Constitution. Individual states also have their own constitutions. Forty-three states provide for the "right to bear arms" in their constitutions. Only seven states (California, Iowa, Maryland, Minnesota, New Jersey, New York, and Wisconsin) do not have constitutional provisions for the "right to bear arms." Only two states, Alaska and Hawaii, mirror the exact words of the Second Amendment of the United States Constitution. Here is what some of the other constitutions say about guns:

Right of the State Lawmakers to Regulate

Nine states give authority to their lawmakers to pass gun control measures. They are Florida, Georgia,

Mississippi, Missouri, Montana, North Carolina, South Carolina, Texas, and Utah.

Right to Protect the Home or Family

Seven state constitutions mention the right to bear arms to protect the family or home. They are Colorado, Delaware, Mississippi, Missouri, Nebraska, New Hampshire, and North Dakota.

Right to Use Guns for Hunting or Recreational Purposes

Five state constitutions reserve the right to use guns for hunting or recreational purposes. They are Delaware, Nebraska, Nevada, New Mexico, and North Dakota.

Provide for Common Defense

The constitutions of Tennessee and Massachusetts limit the right to bear arms for the common good.

Restrict Citizen Militias

The constitutions of two states, Arizona and Washington, prohibit nongovernment military groups.

The constitutions of the first thirteen colonies differ from state constitutions written later in the history of this country. Of the seven state constitutions that do not have "right to bear arms" provisions, three (Maryland, New Jersey, and New York) were among the original thirteen colonies.

- Three state constitutions (North Carolina, South Carolina, and Virginia) have language similar to the Second Amendment.

• Four state constitutions provide for the right to bear arms for self-defense. They are Connecticut, Delaware, New Hampshire, and Pennsylvania.

• Two state constitutions (Georgia and North Carolina) specifically grant their lawmakers the right to pass firearm laws.

State Firearm Laws

Each state has its own firearm laws. State lawmakers make these laws. States with large populations, such as New York, Illinois, and California, often have very restrictive gun laws. State lawmakers can change from election to election. Because of this, gun laws can change too. If you are not sure what laws your state or city has, you can check with the police department in your city or the county sheriff in order to find out.

Here are some current state gun laws. What is your opinion about them?

Gun Identification

Should all gun owners be required to have an owner identification card? Only a few states require the owner of a handgun or a long gun to have an owner identification card. Such identification cards would trace firearms to the owner.

Carrying Firearms in Plain View

Should ordinary citizens be allowed to carry a gun? In some states it is legal for a person to carry a gun in plain view.[1]

Concealed-Weapon Laws

Concealed-weapon laws allow a person to have a gun, yet hide it so no one knows a gun is carried. Who should be allowed to have a concealed weapon? Should this be limited to police detectives? Security officers may have concealed weapons. Banks may have guards with concealed guns. Police detectives may carry concealed weapons so no one even knows they are officers.

Arizona, North Dakota, Washington, Georgia, and Montana allow citizens to carry concealed weapons with few restrictions. Other states require an occupational need before a permit to have a concealed weapon is given. Some states prohibit concealed weapons altogether. Illinois issues no permit to carry a concealed weapon. Thirty-one states have right-to-carry laws permitting citizens to carry a concealed firearm. Twenty-two states have adopted such laws in the last decade, eleven in 1995 and 1996.

Registration of Guns

Should guns be registered? Some states require the registration of a handgun. Large metropolitan areas such as Chicago and New York City require the registration of all guns.

Purchase Permits

Should a person be required to have a license to buy a handgun? Fourteen states require a license or permit to purchase a handgun. Some require a waiting period to purchase. A waiting period allows a law-enforcement office to check whether that person is a felon. If that person is less than twenty-one or has committed a felony, the permit will not be issued.

Only six states and the District of Columbia require a permit to purchase a long gun. These states are Hawaii, Illinois, Michigan, Minnesota, New Jersey, and New York.

Some states require firearms being transported to be in a gun case and to be unloaded. Other states allow a firearm to be transported in plain view (top). A police detective carries a concealed handgun as part of his job (bottom). Some states grant the right of a person to have a concealed weapon only if the person's job requires it.

Waiting Periods

Should there be waiting periods to purchase guns? Several states have waiting periods to purchase guns. In California a person must wait fifteen days before purchasing either a long gun or a handgun. Under the 1993 Brady Act, a five-day waiting period to purchase a handgun became the law in all states. In some cases the state law is moot because a longer period is required.

Several states have the capability to do an instant background check on those wanting to purchase a firearm. If a person is a felon, this information will show up on the background check. By November 30, 1998, all states are required to voluntary instant background-check systems. Unfortunately such systems are expensive to install and maintain.

Children and Guns

Do you agree with restrictions on children having guns? Federal laws restrict federal firearm licensees from selling long guns to minors, those who are less than eighteen years of age. Anyone who is not yet twenty-one cannot buy a handgun.

Safe Storage of Firearms Away From Children

Do you think people should be permitted to keep guns in their homes? If yes, how should those guns be stored so children will not be hurt? There are a shocking number of children who find guns and play with them. Some of those innocent playtimes result in the death of a child. Several states have laws that require the safe storage of firearms when children are present. For example, California laws require safe storage of firearms where children under fourteen might gain access to them.

Minnesota requires all gun sellers to post a warning sign. "It is unlawful to store or leave a loaded firearm where a child under fourteen can obtain access." Minnesota law also makes it illegal for anyone to give a youth under the age of eighteen a firearm unless the parents, guardian, or police consent.

School Buildings

Should guns be allowed in schools or on the playgrounds? Sounds scary, doesn't it? Imagine going to school and wondering whether other students have guns. In several states there are laws that make it a crime to have a gun on school property or on a school bus.

Disqualification Laws

Who should not be allowed to have a gun? If you are not permitted to compete in a certain sporting event, it may be because you are disqualified for a good reason. In the same way, there are certain people who are disqualified from owning firearms. Every state in the United States disqualifies certain people. They may be felons, drug addicts, mental patients, or minors. For a school project on the Second Amendment, you may want to invite your local police chief to explain the firearm laws of your state and city. Ask who is disqualified from having a firearm.

Local Gun Laws

Most states, (forty of them), have just one set of firearm laws that apply to everyone in that state. Certain states, however, allow local governments to make their own gun laws. For example, some cities in

Illinois, New York, and California have their own city laws that are more restrictive than state laws.

In 1981, the city of Morton Grove, Illinois, led the way in banning all handguns, sawed-off shotguns, and machine guns. Several other cities in Illinois followed Morton Grove's example. The city of Evanston, for instance, also prohibited the sale of all firearms.

New York City requires permits to purchase any firearm, and all firearms have to be registered. Permits to carry rifles, shotguns, and handguns are also required. For example, in order to have a rifle in New York City, a person must submit four photos, be fingerprinted, and submit two statements of good character. New York City has some of the most restrictive gun laws in the country. It is also the most populous city in the United States.

In January 1989, the use of an assault weapon in the murder of innocent schoolchildren in Stockton, California, shocked the nation. As a result, several cities in California banned assault weapons. Weapons like the AK-47, Uzi, and AR-15 were banned.

Many cities have passed laws banning guns, but in 1982, Kennesaw, Georgia, did the exact opposite. This town of some eighty-five hundred people passed a law requiring every head of household residing in the city limits of the City of Kennesaw to maintain a firearm and ammunition. Instead of giving up their firearms, this town required their citizens to take up arms.

Surrendering Guns

Several cities, in an effort to ban guns, passed laws requiring citizens to surrender their guns. The courts ruled that such laws were not valid. Voluntary gun surrender programs have proved more successful. In those programs the people willingly surrender their guns. As varied as the colors in a rainbow, the laws of state and local governments across this nation reflect different attitudes about guns and the freedom to own them.

State Court Decisions

In a trial, witnesses tell their story. Based on what the witnesses say, a judge or jury decides the outcome. If one or both of the parties in that trial are not satisfied with the decision, an appeal may be made. Each state has one court that has the power to make a final decision. The same system exists in the federal courts, where the United States Supreme Court is the final authority.

Unlike the United States Supreme Court, whose decisions affect the whole country, each state court makes decisions for its state only. The following state court cases are only examples. Your state may differ from the outcomes written here. In each case, think about whether you agree with the decision of the court. If not, think about how you might have decided the case if you were the judge.

Not all people have a right to purchase or possess firearms. A trial court found Patrick Owenby to be mentally ill. There was evidence to support his commitment to a mental institution. On one occasion he entered the home of Tony Zamora, held an ax behind Zamora's back, and tried to kill him. When the police officer arrived, Owenby lunged for the officer's gun.

This case was heard in Oregon, where there was a law that restricted the mentally ill from having a gun. The court said such a law did not violate the state constitutional right to bear arms. The court concluded that the state legislature could place reasonable limitations on the right to own a gun.[2]

A gun seller can be responsible for injuries that result from a gun sold. Most court cases hold that the gun seller cannot be held responsible for damage caused by that gun. However, in certain instances where a seller is negligent in checking the qualifications of the person purchasing the gun, the gun dealer may be responsible for injury. For example, if a felon, mentally ill person, or minor purchases a gun, the dealer may be responsible if the dealer did not use proper care in making the sale. Also if a gun dealer sells a handgun to someone who is not yet twenty-one, that dealer may be negligent and liable for injuries. What if a gun dealer sells a gun to a "lawful purchaser" yet knows the gun will be used by someone who is not qualified to purchase a gun? Would the dealer be liable if someone were injured? Certain cases have indicated that it is possible the dealer could be liable.

In certain states a person does not have a constitutional right to carry a loaded weapon on him- or herself or in a car. Berton Atkinson of Minnesota filed for a permit to carry a loaded pistol in the glove compartment of his car. He traveled long distances from home and wanted a gun accessible. He was denied a permit.

Minnesota law required a permit to carry a handgun. The Minnesota Supreme Court agreed with the denial of Atkinson's request for a permit. The court stated that there is not an absolute constitutional right to carry a loaded gun on a public highway. The court also concluded that travel alone was not a personal safety hazard.[3]

A person has a right to possess a weapon for self-protection in certain situations. Joseph Schubert received a letter with the words "Pig, you are dead" on it. He suspected his brother had sent it. Schubert applied for a handgun permit. In his request, Schubert claimed that his brother had also once fired a rifle at his van and ordered him away from their mother's home. Fearing for his life, Schubert claimed he needed to carry a gun to protect himself.

In 1980, the Indiana Court of Appeals said that self-protection was a proper reason to have a handgun and the permit should not be denied.[4]

Gun control laws do not violate the Second Amendment right to bear arms. Lee A. Sandidge was convicted of carrying a pistol without a license. This violated the laws of the District of Columbia. He was sentenced to one to ten years of imprisonment. Then the sentence was suspended, and he was placed on a two-year probationary term. He was also fined $150. He appealed. Sandidge claimed that District of Columbia laws violated his constitutional right to keep and bear arms. The court did not agree with Sandidge. It held that the District of Columbia had a right to regulate the use and possession of guns.[5]

The maker of a handgun is not responsible for crimes committed with one of its firearms. A Maryland appellate court ruled that a manufacturer is not responsible for how a handgun is used, any more than a car manufacturer is responsible for a car that is used in an inappropriate way. The court said that a handgun is not defective because it can inflict harm. The court also said that to impose liability on manufacturers for the misuse of handguns would be contrary to public policy.[6]

A state can restrict the right of a person to use a gun to hunt. Voigt McKinley Barnhardt was found guilty of hunting elk without a rifle tag. He claimed that his Second Amendment constitutional right to bear arms was violated. The court disagreed. This

1984 decision of an Oregon court gave the state government the authority to regulate and restrict hunting within its state boundaries.[7]

A state can prohibit a private militia. The United States Constitution provides that states can maintain official militias. Based on this authority, states have National Guard units. Unofficial non governmental military groups also exist, however. Do members of these unofficial groups have a right to meet, use arms, and perform drills?

Ted E. Oakes was a member of an unofficial Kansas militia known as the Posse Comitatus. He claimed that because he was a member of a militia, he did not have to register his firearm or comply with other firearm laws. The court held that the Second Amendment did not protect his right to keep an unregistered firearm. It also held that his membership in an unofficial militia did not give him those privileges.[8] With very few exceptions, state courts have upheld the right of their lawmakers to pass firearm laws that restrict ownership and use of firearms.

Court Rulings on Local Ordinances

Rosetta C. Scales carried a .38-caliber Arminius Titan Tiger without gun owner identification. She violated an East Cleveland, Ohio, municipal ordinance in doing so. She was found guilty and fined. Her gun was taken from her and destroyed. Scales took her case to court. She argued that the law was unconstitutional.

The court said the city of East Cleveland could require handgun-owner identification cards. It also said the Second Amendment did not give an absolute right to own a gun without restrictions. In essence, Ohio approved the right of local governments to regulate the use of firearms within their limits.[9]

Portland, Oregon, had a city ordinance that prohibited appearing in a public place with a loaded gun. Michael Boyce appealed when he was found guilty. The appeal's court affirmed the lower-court decision. The Oregon Court of Appeals said the city could regulate how guns were used. The court said a city could pass laws that protect its citizens.[10]

A municipality can ban handguns completely. The Morton Grove, Illinois, Ordinance 81-11, of June 8, 1981, said, "No person shall possess, in the Village . . . any handgun, unless the same has been rendered permanently inoperative." An ordinance of this kind banning handguns entirely was a first in this country. Two court challenges were made. The court gave the same decision in each. "Not every right secured by the state or federal constitution is fundamental. The right to bear arms has never been thought to be an individual right."[11]

State gun laws vary from state to state, and they are complex and difficult to understand. What might be perfectly legal in rural Montana might be a crime in New York City. What might have influenced the federal government to pass uniform laws that apply to all states? Could it have been that the laws from state to state were so different? What do you think?

8

Arguments Against Gun Control

Charlie Mikos of Bensalem, Pennsylvania, had just gone to bed when he was roused by his daughter's screams and the sounds of a struggle. Running downstairs, he found a man holding what later turned out to be a stun gun to her head. Grabbing his pistol, Mikos pointed it at the man, convinced him to cease his assault, and held him for the police.[1]

The Arguments

Others tell stories like this one in defense of guns, and how they have used them to protect their families. Those who oppose gun control fear that any limitation on the right to bear arms will lead to more and more restrictions. Those who oppose gun control use the following arguments:

The Second Amendment gives each American the right to "keep and bear arms." Those who support the right to possess a gun point out that the Second

Amendment to the United States Constitution gives each American the right to keep and bear arms. These are some of their views:

1. Many state constitutions grant the right for an individual citizen to possess guns.

2. To take away the individual right to have guns is no different from the attempt of the British to "disarm" the colonists during the Revolutionary War.

3. The Bill of Rights is about individual freedoms such as freedom of speech, press, and religion, and the right to a trial by jury. The freedom to have a gun is also an individual freedom.

4. "Militia" refers to all able-bodied males, not just the National Guard.

The Founding Fathers wanted firearms available. They feared a powerful federal government. Those who oppose gun control quote the Founding Fathers. Here is what several of those founders said about guns.

"That a well regulated militia, composed of the body of the people, trained to arms, is the proper, natural, and safe defence of a free state." George Mason, Virginia Declaration of Rights, June 12, 1776.[2]

"No freeman shall be debarred the use of arms." Thomas Jefferson, Proposals for the Virginia Constitution.[3]

"Americans possess [the advantage of being armed] over the people of almost every other nation, [whose] governments are afraid to trust the people with arms." James Madison, in support of private ownership of arms.[4]

The Founding Fathers distrusted standing armies—full-time professional military run by the government. The British used standing armies. For this reason, these founders supported local militias to oppose a powerful federal government.

Police cannot be everywhere. Those in favor of an individual's right to own a gun say people have the right to protect themselves. They claim that includes the right to have a gun. They claim that police often come to the scene of a crime too late, and that protection of one's property and home is the duty of every citizen. Law enforcement officers cannot be expected to provide around-the-clock protection.

Citizens in the United States own an estimated 80 million handguns. At least half of those owners claim they own a handgun for safety and protection. It is impossible to know exactly how many times firearms have been used in self-defense. Criminologist Gary Kleck claims that each year guns are used 2.5 million times for self-protection.[5] Victims who use a gun are less likely to be attacked. They are also less likely to suffer injury.[6]

Accidental firearm deaths are decreasing. Those opposed to gun control show statistics in support of their argument that firearm deaths are decreasing. From 1974 to 1996, unintentional firearm-injury deaths decreased from 2,513 to 1,400.[7]

In 1994, motor vehicle accidents were the leading cause of unintentional-injury deaths for ages one through twenty-four. Motor vehicle accident deaths claimed 13,638 for that age group, while firearms took only 723.[8]

In 1995, firearms ranked seventh as the cause of accidental deaths, after motor vehicles, falls, poisoning, drowning, fires or burns, and choking.

ACCIDENTAL DEATHS, 1996	
TYPE	**NUMBER**
Motor Vehicle	43,300
Falls	14,100
Poisoning (including drugs)	9,800
Drowning	3,900
Fires, Burns	3,200
Suffocation	3,000
Firearms	**1,400**[9]

Gun control does not reduce crime. Gun groups claim that all the firearm laws in the world will not reduce crime. They argue that longer prison terms are a better way to stop crime. These groups also oppose more laws that restrict the right to possess guns. Some of the restrictions opposed are registration, licensing, background checks, and mandatory waiting periods. Does gun control reduce crime? Those who oppose gun control say gun control does not stop crime.

New York City has restrictive gun control laws. In 1967, New York approved a rifle and shotgun registration law. The fee to register a gun was three dollars. Today that fee is fifty-five dollars. After the law was passed, crime rose in New York City.[10]

In 1991, New York City passed a law that banned the private possession of certain semiautomatic guns. Citizens were required to do one of three things: (1) take the guns out of the city limits; (2) make the guns inoperable (unusable); or (3) surrender them to law enforcement.[11]

Despite these laws, crime continued to rise. Gun advocates claim the New York City story is not unusual. They say strict guns laws do not guarantee that crime will go down. In fact, they believe it may have the opposite effect.

In 1987, Florida passed a law that allowed for licensed persons to carry a concealed firearm. Felons would be denied such a license, according to federal law.[12] Gun control supporters opposed this law, and Florida was labeled the "Gunshine state."

Florida has issued over 330,000 permits to carry a concealed firearm. Gun advocates say the law has successfully controlled crime. The state's murder rate has gone down 27 percent. Violent crime has risen only 11.9 percent, while nationwide violent crime has risen 17.4 percent.

Georgia, Indiana, Maine, New Hampshire, North Dakota, South Dakota, and Washington have laws similar to Florida's law. Vermont allows the right to carry a firearm without a license or permit.[13]

In the 1960s, Washington, D.C., required police approval to possess a handgun. In 1976, a handgun ban passed. A 1994 report showed that 304 of the city's 309 firearm homicides were committed with handguns. The homicide rate in this city is about 75 per one hundred thousand. The national rate is only 9.5 per one hundred thousand.

Gun advocates believe residents in the Washington, D.C., area need gun protection. They argue that restrictions on private ownership of guns there have resulted in higher crime. "What has the gun control law done to keep criminals from getting guns? Absolutely nothing. . . . [City residents] ought to have the opportunity to have a handgun." These are the words of a former Washington, D.C., police chief.[14]

Does gun control stop crime? Researchers opposed to gun control quote the following statistics:

• Since the ban on handguns in Washington, D.C., the murder rate has tripled.

• Since South Carolina limited handgun sales to one per month per person, violent crime rose more than 100 percent.

• California has a fifteen-day waiting period on handgun sales, and in 1989 banned assault weapons. This state has a homicide rate 38 percent higher than the rest of the country.[15]

• In 1982, Kennesaw, Georgia, passed a law that required all heads of households keep a firearm in the house.[16] Since that time crime has decreased 16 percent, while the population has almost doubled.[17]

Polls mislead. Polls show that people favor stricter firearm laws. Gun advocates argue that when asked, citizens do not even know any of the gun laws that are currently on the books. Gun advocates quote other polls that show most people

• oppose registration of firearms;

• oppose police deciding who should own guns; and

• do not believe stricter gun control will prevent criminals from getting guns.[18]

Guns are needed for self-protection. Studies show that criminals fear armed citizens. Having a gun reduces the chance of robberies, rapes, and assaults.[19] Gun advocates want the availability of guns to protect home, family, and others. A police officer stopped a carload of teenagers in Salem, Connecticut. The youths scuffled with the officer. An ordinary citizen saw the problem, retrieved his pistol, and stood on his

Each year over 16 million people find pleasure in hunting outdoors. Hunters have long been advocates for less gun control. This hunter displays a twelve-gauge Winchester shotgun used to hunt pheasant.

lawn with his gun in hand. The young people calmed down when they saw the citizen with a handgun.[20]

Gun control affects hunting. There are between 16 million and 20 million recreational hunters in the United States. Each year millions of recreational hunting licenses are sold to hunters. Many hunters oppose gun control. They claim registration and licensing of guns increases the cost of hunting and that a sport that could be enjoyed by many will soon be reserved only for the wealthy. When regulations are increased on sales and manufacturing of guns, those costs are passed on to buyers.

Hunters claim an overabundance of wild animals threatens humans, and hunting is good for an ecological balance. Hunters fear that some gun control only leads to more restrictive gun control. They want to protect their right to hunt and to use the guns and ammunition of their own choice.

The best way to control crime is to lock up criminals, not take away guns from law-abiding citizens. "Guns don't kill, people do." This is the slogan of those who oppose gun control. They claim more emphasis should be placed on punishing criminals, instead of taking guns away from law-abiding citizens. One organization recommends reform of the criminal justice system. It suggests the following five ways:

1. **Put criminals in prison.** Prisons are expensive to maintain. As a result, over 71 percent of the criminals sentenced are free on parole or probation. More prisons should be built to house criminals.

2. **Impose adequate sentences.** Criminals serve an average of only one third of their sentence before being let out on parole. The average prison time for murder is only 7.7 years; for rape 4.6; and robbery, 3.3. Violent criminals should serve 85 percent of their sentence time before parole.

3. **Get hard on repeat offenders.** Repeat criminals may commit as many as 237 crimes per year. Many people are hurt, killed, or victimized. Stiffer laws are needed to deal with repeat criminals.

4. **Make juveniles who commit adult crimes serve adult time.** Youth crimes are on the rise. Arrests for youth involved in murder, rape,

robbery, and aggravated assault went from 91,317 in 1990 to 119,678 in 1993, an increase of more than 30 percent in three years. Only 1.5 percent of juvenile offenders served time.

5. **Involve victims in the sentencing process.** Victims give testimony at the trial, but they are rarely asked what they think the sentence should be. These reforms would give victims a chance to say what they believe would be a fair sentence.[21]

Gun Organizations

There are several organizations that support the right of individuals to own guns. The best-known organization is the National Rifle Association (NRA), which was founded in 1871. Here are some of its purposes:

• To encourage hunting

• To support police officers

• To defend the view that the Second Amendment gives individuals the right to have firearms

• To provide gun safety training[22]

Organizations such as the Citizens Committee for the Right to Keep and Bear Arms and the Second Amendment Foundation also oppose gun control. In 1990, the NRA began a gun safety program for children. It is called "Learn Gun Safety with Eddie Eagle." The program teaches that *guns are not toys.* It also teaches basic gun safety so you will know what to do in case you come in contact with a gun. For example, if you see a gun, do the following:

1. Stop.

2. Don't touch.

3. Leave the area.

4. Tell an adult.[23]

The NRA works closely with 4-H Clubs, Boy Scouts, and other community organizations to teach youth gun safety. Gun safety training is important for everyone. Even if your home does not have guns, other homes do. There may be as many as 212 million firearms possessed by citizens of the United States.[24] The Eddie Eagle program also teaches that a gun should be used only when an adult is supervising. The following firearm safety rules are taught:

1. Always keep the gun pointed in a safe direction.

2. Always keep your finger off the trigger until ready to shoot.

3. Always keep the gun unloaded until ready to use.[25]

Those who oppose gun control want to keep guns in the hands of private citizens. They believe the Second Amendment guarantees this right to law-abiding people. They say gun control laws have had little effect in controlling crime, and the best way to control crime is to get tough on criminals. The rights of hunting, collecting guns, and protecting yourself against crime are all freedoms gun advocates say are a part of the Second Amendment. Before you make up your mind, listen to what those who support gun control have to say.

9

Gun Control and Those Who Support It

The following example illustrates the arguments of many people who support gun control:

> At 8:00 P.M. Saturday evening, I dropped my son and his friend off at a party. This is the last time I saw his face. He said, "Thanks, Dad." At 11:30 P.M. he called to say the music got started a little late. He asked if he could stay later. We settled on 12:30. He was shot at 12:15 A.M. He was an innocent victim caught in the crossfire of a gang shooting. When I came to pick him up at 12:30, it was too late.
>
> I personally am counting on this political system, on the federal system that must fight back. The Federal Government is the only one with the power to control the arms industry. I beg, plead, and demand that the arms industry be regulated so dealers are made to pay the costs for this great tragedy.[1]

Tom Vandenberk's son was one of 38,166 people who died in 1994 in the United States from gunshot wounds.[2] Motor vehicle deaths annually total about 43,000.[3] Individual Americans own over two hundred million firearms. Guns are a big business. Those who support gun control want restrictions on ownership and use. Here are some of their reasons:

The Arguments

Guns are not an absolute constitutional right. Gun control advocates say the Second Amendment is not about the right of the individual to have a gun. It is about the right of each state to operate its own militia. Advocates quote Supreme Court decisions to back up this understanding of the Second Amendment. A 1939 Supreme Court decision said the obvious purpose of the Second Amendment was to assure the continuation and effectiveness of the state militia forces.[4]

Gun control advocates challenge NRA views that the Second Amendment is about the right of an individual to own a gun. Former Chief Justice Warren Burger, of the United States Supreme Court, after he retired from his seat on the Supreme Court, took a stand on the issue of gun control. He said that the NRA has perpetrated a "fraud on the American public," and has distorted the text, history, and judicial interpretation of the Second Amendment.[5] He continued, "Is there any question that a citizen has the right to own and keep an automobile? Yet we accept the state's power to regulate its purchase and to license the vehicle and its driver. Should guns be any different?"[6]

Gun control supporters look to a long history of court decisions about this amendment. The courts have said the government, both federal and state, has a right to limit the private ownership of guns.

Firearm death numbers are shocking. Of 38,166 firearm deaths in 1994, 11,823 involved young people. Of those 11, 823 deaths, 10,954 were between the ages of fifteen and twenty-four; 762 were between ages of five and fourteen; and 107 were under five years of age.[7]

Here is a further breakdown of firearm deaths of young people:[8]

From those statistics, of all the youth firearm deaths, 63 percent were murder; 28 percent were suicides; 7 percent were accidents; and 2 percent were from unknown causes.

Suicide deaths are on the rise among young people. Each year many young people die of suicide. Maybe you know of someone in your school who committed suicide. In many suicide cases, a firearm is used. In a child custody case in Minnesota, both the mom and

YOUTH FIREARM DEATHS, 1994		
AGES	**TYPE**	**NUMBER**
15–24	All Deaths	10,954
	Accident	540
	Suicide	3,344
	Murder	6,811
	Unknown	189
5–14	All Deaths	762
	Accident	151
	Suicide	188
	Murder	395
	Unknown	28
Under 5	All Deaths	107
	Accident	34
	Suicide	0
	Murder	71
	Unknown	2

the dad wanted custody of their son. The case was brought to court. Before a decision could be made by the court, the sixteen-year-old boy made a tragic decision. While home alone, he took his hunting shotgun and ended his life.

Did You Know?

- Suicide attempts with firearms almost always result in death.[9]

- Among teen suicides, males used a gun in 65 percent of the cases; females, in 47 percent of the cases.[10]

- Suicide is on the increase among youth.[11]

- Most teen suicides are impulsive, with little or no planning. Seventy percent occur at home.[12]

- Thirty-two percent of youth firearm deaths are suicides. This is an increase of 4 percent from 1993.[13]

Guns In the Home are Dangerous

- A twelve-year-old girl was talking with her friend at dusk over her back fence when she heard some popping noises. She realized it might be guns and turned to run. She was shot in the shoulder.[14]

- A seven-year-old boy was taking a bath. His sixteen-year-old brother came home with a handgun. The seven-year-old asked to see the gun. The older boy handed it to him. The seven-year-old shot himself in the stomach and died in the hospital.[15]

- A four-year-old boy was shot by a stray bullet while in his grandmother's dining room. The bullet lodged in his brain. He lived only because of the hard work of his surgeon.[16]

Former Surgeon General Joycelyn Elders expressed concern about guns in the home: At times when parents are not home, 1.2 million elementary-age children have access to guns in their home.[17] According to Dr. Arthur L. Kellermann, director of the Center for Injury Control in Atlanta, Georgia, "Homes with guns are 4.8 times more likely to be the scene of a suicide and 2.7 times more likely to be the scene of a homicide than comparable homes without guns."[18]

Although many believe a gun is needed for self-defense, gun control supporters say guns increase the chance of injury or death to family members. They report: "From 1987–1990, victims used firearms to protect themselves in fewer than one percent of all violent offenses."[19] Several states now require guns to be locked up when children are in the home. Do you think that is a reasonable requirement?

There are too many guns in schools. "It is easier for some of our children to obtain a gun than it is to find a good friend, a good teacher, a good school, or even a good minister." These words of former Surgeon General Joycelyn Elders signal a national problem. She also said, "It is estimated that 135,000 children take guns to school every day. A nationwide survey of high school students found that one in twenty students had carried a gun, usually a handgun, during the past month."[20]

Seven percent of New York City high school students carry a handgun to school.[21]

A 1993 survey of public high school students in a suburban area found that 18 percent possessed a handgun.[22]

A survey of sixth- to twelfth-grade students indicated that they knew where to get a gun. Two thirds of those surveyed said they could get a gun within twenty-four hours.[23] Middle school students possessed 853 of the 1,249 weapons found in public schools in Virginia during a one-year period.[24] A United States senator said: "We recently had a case where a five-year-old, believe it or not, brought a handgun to school."[25]

The cost of treating one gunshot wound could send a child to college for a year. Those who support gun control say the medical cost of gun violence is staggering. One senator said, "To treat a child for a bullet wound costs an average of $14,000."[26] That is about the cost of one year of college.

Consider the following costs:

- It costs about $4 billion a year to treat gun-related injuries in the United States.[27]

- A gun injury that leads to death can cost $373,000 to treat.[28]

- "The yearly direct cost of medical care for victims of firearm injuries exceeds one billion dollars. Loss of ability to work and the need for other medical care may be as high as 15 billion dollars annually."[29]

Gun violence costs money, pain, suffering, and loss of life. Many doctors and medical people believe guns should not be kept in a home where there are children.

Gun Control Works

The Brady Act

The intent of the law, which went into effect in February 1994, was to stop felons and drug offenders from buying handguns. A five-day waiting period gave time to law enforcement officials to do a check on the person applying to purchase a handgun. The Supreme Court has rendered a decision that the required background checks by state law enforcement officers are unconstitutional. The 1997 decision of *Printz v. United States* did not invalidate the five-day waiting period, but did reduce the background check to a voluntary system nationwide.[30] A state, however, can still require a background check.

Among those denied handguns in the first eleven months of the Brady Act were 4,365 convicted felons. Others who were not allowed to buy handguns were fugitives, illegal drug users, juveniles, and persons

James and Sarah Brady are strong gun control advocates. The Brady Law, passed in 1993, was named after James Brady, who was wounded in an assassination attempt on President Reagan in 1981.

who had been involved in domestic threats or harassment or alleged stalking.[31]

The Assault Weapons Ban

In 1994, nineteen types of semiautomatic assault weapons were banned. Among them were the Uzi, AK-47, and TEC-9. This particular law has been in effect a short time. Those who claim this law works report that 18 percent fewer assault weapons were traced to crime in 1995 than in 1994.[32]

Assault weapons have been used in many violent crimes. On January 17, 1989, Patrick Purdy killed five small children and wounded twenty-nine others, including a teacher at an elementary school in Stockton, California. He used a version of the AK-47 assault rifle. He fired 106 rounds in less than two minutes. The gun had been purchased legally.

In July 1993, Gian Luigi Ferri killed eight people and wounded six at a San Francisco law office. He was using three TEC DC-9 assault pistols. The guns had been purchased in Las Vegas, Nevada. Gun control advocates believe that the assault weapons ban has had and will continue to have a positive effect on crime control.

Other Gun Control Laws

In July 1993, the state of Virginia passed a gun law entitled "One Gun a Month." It limits a person to one handgun purchase per month. This has reduced the number of handguns in circulation in Virginia.[33] It has also reduced illegal sales of guns to other states.

Gun control supporters also look to other countries. They claim the United States does not have effective gun control laws and that is one reason for the increase

A 1994 law of Congress prohibits certain assault weapons. This Tec-9 Mini and Tec-9 were among them.

in violent crime in the United States. The number of handgun murders in countries such as Australia, Japan, Great Britain, Switzerland, Sweden, and Canada rarely is over one hundred per year.

For example, in 1992 Japan had only sixty handgun murders. In that same year, there were about thirteen thousand in the United States. Japan's population is approximately half that of the United States. Japan has very restrictive gun laws. Handguns are almost totally banned for private ownership. Japan has the lowest known murder rate in the world.[34]

The shooting deaths of sixteen kindergarten children and their teacher in Dunblane, Scotland, in 1996 prompted British lawmakers to consider a complete ban on handguns. In 1995, Great Britain had 409,000 firearms, with a total of 77 firearm murders. The United States has over 200 million firearms, with a total of 13,673 firearm murders.[35]

Canada has restrictive gun control laws. Handguns are banned. A study of Seattle, Washington, and Vancouver, British Columbia, revealed that assaults involving firearms were eight times higher in Seattle than in Vancouver. Yet the cities are comparable in size. Seattle has very few firearm restrictions, whereas Vancouver's laws are strict.[36] Those who advocate stricter gun control look to Canada, Great Britain, and Japan as proof that gun control can also mean crime control.

Necessity of Federal Laws

A president of a police organization said, "What we need is the type of legislation that is uniform throughout the country. There is a lack of continuity of laws."[37] Gun control advocates want federal laws that apply to everyone. Does gun control mean crime control? Gun control proponents say gun laws can make a difference. In two years, more people in the United States died from firearms than died in the entire Vietnam War. Both sides might agree that young people are at risk. Many young children below the age of eight cannot tell a real gun from a toy gun. And the odds are that more suicides will occur in homes with guns than in those without.[38] Keeping a gun at home triples the risk that a homicide will be committed in the home.[39] What are we as a nation going to do? What can you do?

Gun Violence—Eight Things You Can Do

Regardless of how many gun control laws there are, guns are a part of American life. It has been that way since the beginning of this country. You may be in favor of Americans' right to own guns or you may be opposed to it. In either case, there are important safety precautions you can take to protect yourself and those around you.

1. *Think about the impact of the violence on television.* "The average child sees 8,000 murders and 100,000 acts of violence on television before entering elementary school."[1] Television is not real. Real guns hurt people forever. A leader for responsible gun laws had this warning: "TV violence certainly is a great problem that we have, the glamorization of weapons."[2]

2. *Keep guns locked up at home.* Guns are dangerous and harmful. Talk to your parents about guns. The American Academy of

Pediatrics "believes handguns should be eliminated from the environment in which children live and play."[3] Statistics show that guns in the home are more likely to be used on a family member than on someone who breaks into the home.

3. *Do not play with or around guns.* Many children have lost their lives playing with guns. Several states require proper storage of firearms so they are kept out of the reach of children. If you see guns in a friend's or neighbor's home that are not safely stored, ask that they be put away, or leave the house.

4. *Encourage your school to educate all young people about guns.* "If I see a gun or anything that looks like a gun, I will not touch it." Would you be willing to make this pledge? A school-based program called STAR (Straight Talk About Risks) encourages young people to make that promise. It also teaches young people to solve problems without threats or violence.[4]

Suppose you are hanging around school with some friends. One of them takes out a gun. What would you do? Discuss your options. Would you like to have education about guns in your school? Talk to a teacher, other classmates, or your principal about gun education in your school. Think of ways to get your school involved. Here are several ideas you might consider. Do a project on violence and guns. Give a report to your social studies class or the whole school. Sponsor a poster contest. Submit the winning entry to a local newspaper for publication. Sponsor a "gun-awareness" day. Have a law enforcement officer, a teacher, or a lawyer speak to your school about guns and crime.

5. *Learn the truth about gun violence.* Answer the following true or false.

- The number of gun deaths and injuries among young people is very low.

- A gun in the home is the best way for a person to protect children and home.

- You are safe if there are guns in your home.

If you answered false to all of these, you are correct.

In the United States, the number of gun deaths among young people is high. About sixteen children die from gunshot wounds each day. Guns cause twice as many deaths as cancer among children.[5] A gun in

Research shows that the United States is the most violent country for children of the twenty-six wealthiest nations in the world. The United States leads in murders, suicides, and gun-related deaths involving children. In most cases, the fatality involves the use of a handgun.

the home increases the risk of murder or suicide. In fact, a firearm in the home is more likely to kill a family member or a friend, than to be used in self-defense.[6] Even though your home may not have a gun, nearly 45 percent of American homes do. Thirty percent of those guns are handguns. If you visit a friend's house where there are guns, you may be in danger.[7]

6. *Learn more about gun buy-back programs.* Voluntary gun turn-in programs have successfully removed firearms from the streets and from private homes. County attorney Michael Freeman ran a successful program in Minneapolis, Minnesota. It was called "Drop Your Guns." Each person who brought a gun to a drop-off place was issued a check for fifty dollars. No questions were asked. Over three hundred thousand dollars of private money supported the project. No tax dollars were used. Over six thousand guns were collected and melted to make a sculpture now on display in the government center in Minneapolis. The public relations person for the project said, "This project is about young people. Our youth deserve a nonviolent society."[8]

7. *Encourage responsible gun use.* How much training and supervision do young people need in order to shoot a gun? Should there be as much training as your state requires to drive an automobile? Would the following be reasonable requirements?

• Adult supervision at all times when a youth below the age of twenty-one uses a handgun, and below the age of eighteen for a shotgun or rifle.

• Required hunting-safety programs for children.

• Warning on all firearms about dangers.

• All firearms be stored in a locked gun box when not in use.[9]

Think about other reasonable laws that would keep you and other children safe. You may want to write or e-mail your state representative or senator or congressperson about ideas for possible laws. Ask your teacher to help, or sponsor a class project.

8. *Use a multiple approach.* Gun control laws alone will not reduce crime. They are only part of the solution to violence. Creating a safe America requires more than firearm laws. Here are some other things that can be done:

• Change attitudes about guns. America changed its attitudes about smoking. Many restaurants now ban smoking. Several airlines are also smoke-free. Smoking is not allowed in many public buildings. Attitudes can be changed about guns too.

• Make certain firearms are stored properly.

• Learn how to resolve problems without fighting.

• Learn more about the laws of your state.

Encourage your school, your church, your community, and your family to make good decisions about guns and violence. There are things you can do. Lives are at stake.

11

Living With the Tension

On September 30, 1996, over forty thousand shoes were displayed on the steps of the United States Capitol in Washington, D.C. They stood as a silent memorial to those who had died from gun-related suicides, murders, and accidents in the past year. Among the shoes were the sandals of a four-year-old girl who lost her life in the cross fire of two street gangs. Her mother said, "I just want to let people know that she should never be forgotten."[1]

The issue of guns and violence is not one that is easily forgotten. Every day we hear of gunshot deaths. New gun laws are introduced in almost every session of Congress. It is unlikely that the issue of gun control will go away.

There are those who see guns as a right the Constitution gives the citizens of this country. They want guns for protection and sport. There are others who want more restrictions on guns. They claim gun control is necessary to protect the public and reduce unnecessary deaths.

The guns of today are quite different from those that were in use when the Constitution was written. Today's guns are easier to load, more accurate, and can fire many more shots in succession than the awkward muskets of Colonial times.

In 1791, the founders of this country could not have anticipated the types of firearms that would be available in the future. The musket of Revolutionary War times was accurate only at close range. It cannot be compared with the weapons of today where hundreds of shots can be fired in a few seconds with great accuracy. These signers of the Constitution could not have anticipated the controversy the Second Amendment would create, especially when its approval at that time came almost without debate.

"A well-regulated militia being necessary to the security of a free state, the right of the people to keep and bear arms shall not be infringed." What can we make of this amendment? The Second Amendment has created more controversy today than it did at the time of its approval. What do those twenty-seven words mean? Do they limit the federal government's interfering with the right of a state to maintain its own militia? Or is there more to this amendment? Does it guarantee the right of law-abiding citizens to possess firearms? Guns and freedom are a Second Amendment issue. But there is much more to this issue than a debate over words. Lives are affected. Many times those lives belong to young people. Whether you support the right to own guns or favor stricter gun control, we as a nation must strive to resolve the issue to make this a safe place for all people.

THE CONSTITUTION OF THE UNITED STATES

The text of the Constitution is presented here. All words are given their modern spelling and capitalization. Brackets [ ] indicate parts that have been changed or set aside by amendments.

Preamble

We the people of the United States, in order to form a more perfect Union, establish justice, insure domestic tranquility, provide for the common defense, promote the general welfare, and secure the blessings of liberty to ourselves and our posterity, do ordain and establish this Constitution for the United States of America.

ARTICLE I
The Legislative Branch

Section 1. All legislative powers herein granted shall be vested in a Congress of the United States, which shall consist of a Senate and House of Representatives.

The House of Representatives

Section 2. (1) The House of Representatives shall be composed of members chosen every second year by the people of the several states, and the electors in each state shall have the qualifications requisite for electors of the most numerous branch of the state legislature.

(2) No person shall be a representative who shall not have attained the age of twenty-five years, and been seven years a citizen of the United States, and who shall not, when elected, be an inhabitant of that state in which he shall be chosen.

(3) Representatives and direct taxes shall be apportioned among the several states which may be included within this Union, according to their respective numbers, [which shall be determined by adding to the whole number of free persons, including those bound to service for a term of years, and excluding Indians not taxed, three-fifths of all other persons]. The actual enumeration shall be made within three years after the first meeting of the Congress of the United States, and within every subsequent term of ten years, in such manner as they shall by law direct. The number of representatives shall not exceed one for every thirty thousand, but each state shall have at least one representative; [and until such enumeration shall be made, the state of New Hampshire shall be entitled to choose three, Massachusetts eight, Rhode Island and Providence Plantations one, Connecticut five, New York six, New Jersey four, Pennsylvania eight, Delaware one, Maryland six, Virginia ten, North Carolina five, South Carolina five, and Georgia three].

(4) When vacancies happen in the representation from any state, the executive authority thereof shall issue writs of election to fill such vacancies.

(5) The House of Representatives shall choose their Speaker and other officers; and shall have the sole power of impeachment.

The Senate

Section 3. (1) The Senate of the United States shall be composed of two senators from each state, [chosen by the legislature thereof,] for six years; and each senator shall have one vote.

(2) Immediately after they shall be assembled in consequence of the first election, they shall be divided as equally as may be into three classes. The seats of the senators of the first class shall be vacated at the expiration of the second year, of the second class at the expiration of the fourth year, and of the third class at the expiration of the sixth year, so that one-third may be chosen every second year; [and if vacancies happen by resignation, or otherwise, during the recess of the legislature of any state, the executive thereof may make temporary appointments until the next meeting of the legislature, which shall then fill such vacancies].

(3) No person shall be a senator who shall not have attained to the age of thirty years, and been nine years a citizen of the United States, and who shall not, when elected, be an inhabitant of that state for which he shall be chosen.

(4) The Vice President of the United States shall be president of the Senate, but shall have no vote, unless they be equally divided.

(5) The Senate shall choose their other officers, and also a president *pro tempore*, in the absence of the Vice President, or when he shall exercise the office of President of the United States.

(6) The Senate shall have the sole power to try all impeachments. When sitting for that purpose, they shall be on oath or affirmation. When the President of the United States is tried, the Chief Justice shall preside: and no person shall be convicted without the concurrence of two-thirds of the members present.

(7) Judgement in cases of impeachment shall not extend further than to removal from office, and disqualification to hold and enjoy any office of honor, trust, or profit under the United States: but the party convicted shall nevertheless be liable and subject to indictment, trial, judgement and punishment, according to law.

Organization of Congress

Section 4. (1) The times, places and manner of holding elections for senators and representatives, shall be prescribed in each state by the legislature thereof; but the Congress may at any time by law make or alter such regulations, [except as to the places of choosing senators].

(2) The Congress shall assemble at least once in every year, [and such meeting shall be on the first Monday in December], unless they shall by law appoint a different day.

Section 5. (1) Each house shall be the judge of the elections, returns and qualifications of its own members, and a majority of each shall constitute a quorum to do business; but a smaller number may adjourn from day to day, and may be authorized to compel the attendance of absent members, in such manner, and under such penalties as each house may provide.

(2) Each house may determine the rules of its proceedings, punish its members for disorderly behavior, and, with the concurrence of two-thirds, expel a member.

(3) Each house shall keep a journal of its proceedings, and from time to time publish the same, excepting such parts as may in their judgement require secrecy; and the yeas and nays of the members of either house on any question shall, at the desire of one-fifth of those present, be entered on the journal.

(4) Neither house, during the session of Congress, shall, without the consent of the other, adjourn for more than three days, nor to any other place than that in which the two houses shall be sitting.

Section 6. (1) The senators and representatives shall receive a compensation for their services, to be ascertained by law, and paid out of the treasury of the United States. They shall in all cases, except treason, felony and breach of the peace, be privileged from arrest during their attendance at the session of their respective houses, and in going to and returning from the same; and for any speech or debate in either house, they shall not be questioned in any other place.

(2) No senator or representative shall, during the time for which he was elected, be appointed to any civil office under the authority of the United States, which shall have been created, or the emoluments whereof shall have been increased during such time; and no person holding any office under the United States shall be a member of either house during his continuance in office.

Section 7. (1) All bills for raising revenue shall originate in the House of Representatives; but the Senate may propose or concur with amendments as on other bills.

(2) Every bill which shall have passed the House of Representatives and the Senate, shall, before it become a law, be presented to the President of the United States; if he approve he shall sign it, but if not he shall return it, with his objections to that house in which it shall have originated, who shall enter the objections at large on their journal, and proceed to reconsider it. If after such reconsideration two-thirds of that house shall agree to pass the bill, it shall be sent, together with the objections, to the other house, by which it shall likewise be reconsidered, and if approved by two-thirds of that house, it shall become a law. But in all such cases the votes of both houses shall be determined by yeas and nays, and the names of the persons voting for and against the bill shall be entered on the journal of each house respectively. If any bill shall not be returned by the President within ten days (Sundays excepted) after it shall have been presented to him, the same shall be a law, in like manner as if he had signed it, unless the Congress by their

adjournment prevent its return, in which case it shall not be a law.

(3) Every order, resolution, or vote to which the concurrence of the Senate and House of Representatives may be necessary (except on a question of adjournment) shall be presented to the President of the United States; and before the same shall take effect, shall be approved by him, or being disapproved by him, shall be repassed by two-thirds of the Senate and House of Representatives, according to the rules and limitations prescribed in the case of a bill.

Powers Granted to Congress

The Congress shall have power:

Section 8. (1) To lay and collect taxes, duties, imposts and excises, to pay the debts and provide for the common defense and general welfare of the United States; but all duties, imposts and excises shall be uniform throughout the United States;

(2) To borrow money on the credit of the United States;

(3) To regulate commerce with foreign nations, and among the several states, and with the Indian tribes;

(4) To establish an uniform rule of naturalization, and uniform laws on the subject of bankruptcies throughout the United States;

(5) To coin money, regulate the value thereof, and of foreign coin, and fix the standard of weights and measures;

(6) To provide for the punishment of counterfeiting the securities and current coin of the United States;

(7) To establish post offices and post roads;

(8) To promote the progress of science and useful arts, by securing for limited times to authors and inventors the exclusive right to their respective writings and discoveries;

(9) To constitute tribunals inferior to the Supreme Court;

(10) To define and punish piracies and felonies committed on the high seas, and offenses against the law of nations;

(11) To declare war, grant letters of marque and reprisal, and make rules concerning captures on land and water;

(12) To raise and support armies, but no appropriation of money to that use shall be for a longer term than two years;

(13) To provide and maintain a navy;

(14) To make rules for the government and regulation of the land and naval forces;

(15) To provide for calling forth the militia to execute the laws of the Union, suppress insurrections and repel invasions;

(16) To provide for organizing, arming, and disciplining the militia, and for governing such part of them as may be employed in the service of the United States, reserving to the states respectively, the appointment of the officers, and the authority of training the militia according to the discipline prescribed by Congress;

(17) To exercise exclusive legislation in all cases whatsoever, over such district (not exceeding ten miles square) as may, by cession of particular states, and the acceptance of Congress, become the seat of the government of the United States, and to exercise like authority over all places purchased by the consent of the legislature of the state in which the same shall be, for the erection of forts, magazines, arsenals, dockyards, and other needful buildings;—And

(18) To make all laws which shall be necessary and proper for carrying into execution the foregoing powers, and all other powers vested by this Constitution in the government of the United States, or in any department or officer thereof.

Powers Forbidden to Congress

Section 9. (1) The migration or importation of such persons as any of the states now existing shall think proper to admit, shall not be prohibited by the Congress prior to the year one thousand eight hundred and eight, but a tax or duty may be imposed on such importation, not exceeding ten dollars for each person.

(2) The privilege of the writ of *habeas corpus* shall not be suspended, unless when in cases of rebellion or invasion the public safety may require it.

(3) No bill of attainder or *ex post facto* law shall be passed.

(4) No capitation, [or other direct,] tax shall be laid, unless in proportion to the census or enumeration herein before directed to be taken.

(5) No tax or duty shall be laid on articles exported from any state.

(6) No preference shall be given by any regulation of commerce or revenue to the ports of one state over those of another: nor shall vessels bound to, or from, one state, be obliged to enter, clear, or pay duties in another.

(7) No money shall be drawn from the treasury, but in consequence of appropriations made by law; and a regular statement and account of the receipts and expenditures of all public money shall be published from time to time.

(8) No title of nobility shall be granted by the United States: And no person holding any office or profit or trust under them, shall, without the consent of the Congress, accept of any present, emolument, office, or title, of any kind whatsoever, from any king, prince, or foreign state.

Powers Forbidden to the States

Section 10. (1) No state shall enter into any treaty, alliance, or confederation; grant letters of marque and reprisal; coin money; emit bills of credit; make any thing but gold and silver coin a tender in payment of debts; pass any bill of attainder, *ex post facto* law, or law impairing the obligation of contracts, or grant any title of nobility.

(2) No state shall, without the consent of the Congress, lay any imposts or duties on imports or exports, except what may be absolutely necessary for executing its inspection laws: and the net produce of all duties and imposts, laid by any state on imports or exports, shall be for the use of the treasury of the United States, and all such laws shall be subject to the revision and control of the Congress.

(3) No state shall, without the consent of Congress, lay any duty of tonnage, keep troops, or ships of war in time of peace, enter into any agreement or compact with another state, or with a foreign power, or engage in war, unless actually invaded, or in such imminent danger as will not admit of delay.

Article II
The Executive Branch

Section 1. (1) The executive power shall be vested in a President of the United States of America. He shall hold his office during the term of four years, and, together with the Vice President, chosen for the same term, be elected as follows:

(2) Each state shall appoint, in such manner as the legislature thereof may direct, a number of electors, equal to the whole number of senators and representatives to which the state may be entitled in the Congress: but no senator or representative, or person holding an office of trust or profit under the United States, shall be appointed an elector.

(3) [The electors shall meet in their respective states, and vote by ballot for two persons, of whom one at least shall not be an inhabitant of the same state with themselves. And they shall make a list of all the persons voted for, and of the number of votes for each; which list they shall sign and certify, and transmit sealed to the seat of government of the United States, directed to the president of the Senate. The president of the Senate shall, in the presence of the Senate and House of Representatives, open all the certificates, and the votes shall then be counted. The person having the greatest number of votes shall be the President, if such number be a majority of the whole number of electors appointed; and if there be more than one who have such majority, and have an equal number of votes, then the House of Representatives shall immediately choose by ballot one of them for President; and if no person have a majority, then from the five highest on the list the said House shall in like manner choose the President. But in choosing the President, the votes shall be taken by states, the representation from each state having one vote; a quorum for this purpose shall consist of a member or members from two-thirds of the states, and a majority of all the states shall be necessary to a choice. In every case, after the choice of the President, the person having the greatest number of votes of the electors shall be the Vice President. But if there should remain two or more who have equal votes, the Senate shall choose from them by ballot the Vice President.]

(4) The Congress may determine the time of choosing the electors, and the day on which they shall give their

votes; which day shall be the same throughout the United States.

(5) No person except a natural-born citizen, or a citizen of the United States, at the time of the adoption of this Constitution, shall be eligible to the office of President; neither shall any person be eligible to that office who shall not have attained to the age of thirty-five years, and been fourteen years a resident within the United States.

(6) In case of the removal of the President from office, or of his death, resignation, or inability to discharge the powers and duties of the said office, the same shall devolve on the Vice President, and the Congress may by law provide for the case of removal, death, resignation, or inability, both of the President and Vice President, declaring what officer shall then act as President, and such officer shall act accordingly, until the disability be removed, or a President shall be elected.

(7) The President shall, at stated times, receive for his services, a compensation, which shall neither be increased nor diminished during the period for which he shall have been elected, and he shall not receive within that period any other emolument from the United States, or any of them.

(8) Before he enter on the execution of his office, he shall take the following oath or affirmation: "I do solemnly swear (or affirm) that I will faithfully execute the office of the President of the United States, and will to the best of my ability, preserve, protect and defend the Constitution of the United States."

Section 2. (1) The President shall be commander-in-chief of the Army and Navy of the United States, and of the militia of the several states, when called into the actual service of the United States; he may require the opinion, in writing, of the principal officer in each of the executive departments, upon any subject relating to the duties of their respective offices, and he shall have power to grant reprieves and pardons for offenses against the United States, except in cases of impeachment.

(2) He shall have power, by and with the advice and consent of the Senate, to make treaties, provided two-thirds of the senators present concur; and he shall nominate, and by and with the advice and consent of the Senate, shall appoint ambassadors, other public ministers and consuls, judges of the Supreme Court, and all other officers of the United States, whose appointments are not herein otherwise provided for, and which shall be established by law: but the Congress may by law vest the appointment of such inferior officers, as they think proper, in the President alone, in the courts of law, or in the heads of departments.

(3) The President shall have the power to fill up all vacancies that may happen during the recess of the Senate, by granting commissions which shall expire at the end of their next session.

Section 3. He shall from time to time give to the Congress information of the state of the Union, and recommend to their consideration such measures as he shall judge necessary and expedient; he may, on extraordinary occasions, convene both houses, or either of them, and in case of disagreement between them, with respect to the time of adjournment, he may adjourn them to such time as he shall think proper; he shall receive ambassadors and other public ministers; he shall take care that the laws be faithfully executed, and shall commission all the officers of the United States.

Section 4. The President, Vice President and all civil officers of the United States, shall be removed from office on impeachment for, and conviction of, treason, bribery, or other high crimes and misdemeanors.

ARTICLE III
The Judicial Branch

Section 1. The judicial power of the United States, shall be vested in one Supreme Court, and in such inferior courts as the Congress may from time to time ordain and establish. The judges, both of the Supreme and inferior courts, shall hold their offices during good behaviour, and shall, at stated times, receive for their services, a compensation, which shall not be diminished during their continuance in office.

Section 2. (1) The judicial power shall extend to all cases, in law and equity, arising under this Constitution, the laws of the United States, and treaties made, or which shall be made, under their authority; —to all cases affecting ambassadors, other public ministers and consuls;—to all cases of admiralty and maritime jurisdiction;—to controversies to which the United States shall be a party;—to controversies between two or more states, [between a state and citizens of another state;], between citizens of different states;—between citizens of the same state claiming lands under grants of different states, and between a state, or the citizens thereof, and foreign states, [citizens or subjects].

(2) In all cases affecting ambassadors, other public ministers and consuls, and those in which a state shall be party, the Supreme Court shall have original jurisdiction. In all the other cases before mentioned, the Supreme Court shall have appellate jurisdiction, both as to law and fact, with such exceptions, and under such regulations as the Congress shall make.

(3) The trial of all crimes, except in cases of impeachment, shall be by jury; and such trial shall be held in the state where the said crimes shall have been committed; but when not committed within any state, the trial shall be at such place or places as the Congress may by law have directed.

Section 3. (1) Treason against the United States, shall consist only in levying war against them, or in adhering to their enemies, giving them aid and comfort. No person shall be convicted of treason unless on the testimony of two witnesses to the same overt act, or on confession in open court.

(2) The Congress shall have power to declare the punishment of treason, but no attainder of treason shall work corruption of blood, or forfeiture, except during the life of the person attainted.

ARTICLE IV
Relation of the States to Each Other

Section 1. Full faith and credit shall be given in each state to the public acts, records, and judicial proceedings of every other state. And the Congress may by general laws prescribe the manner in which such acts, records and proceedings shall be proved, and the effect thereof.

Section 2. (1) The citizens of each state shall be entitled to all privileges and immunities of citizens in the several states.

(2) A person charged in any state with treason, felony, or other crime, who shall flee justice, and be found in another state, shall on demand of the executive authority of the state from which he fled, be delivered up, to be removed to the state having jurisdiction of the crime.

(3) [No person held to service or labor in one state, under the laws thereof, escaping into another, shall, in consequence of any law or regulation therein, be discharged from such service or labor, but shall be delivered up on claim of the party to whom such service or labor may be due.]

Federal-State Relations

Section 3. (1) New states may be admitted by the Congress into this Union; but no new state shall be formed or erected within the jurisdiction of any other state, nor any state be formed by the junction of two or more states, without the consent of the legislatures of the states concerned as well as of the Congress.

(2) The Congress shall have power to dispose of and make all needful rules and regulations respecting the territory or other property belonging to the United States; and nothing in this Constitution shall be so construed as to prejudice any claims of the United States, or of any particular state.

Section 4. The United States shall guarantee to every state in this Union a republican form of government, and shall protect each of them against invasion; and on application of the legislature, or of the executive (when the legislature cannot be convened), against domestic violence.

ARTICLE V
Amending the Constitution

The Congress, whenever two-thirds of both houses shall deem it necessary, shall propose amendments to this Constitution, or, on the application of the legislatures of two-thirds of the several states, shall call a convention for proposing amendments, which, in either case, shall be valid to all intents and purposes, as part of this Constitution, when ratified by the legislatures of three-fourths of the several states, or by conventions in three-fourths thereof, as the one or the other mode of ratification may be proposed by the Congress; provided [that no amendment which may be made prior to the year one thousand eight hundred and eight, shall in any manner affect the first and fourth clauses in the ninth section of the first article; and] that no state, without its consent, shall be deprived of its equal suffrage in the Senate.

ARTICLE VI
National Debts

(1) All debts contracted and engagements entered into, before the adoption of this Constitution, shall be as

valid against the United States under this Constitution, as under the Confederation.

Supremacy of the National Government

(2) This Constitution, and the laws of the United States which shall be made in pursuance thereof; and all treaties made, or which shall be made, under the authority of the United States shall be the supreme law of the land; and the judges in every state shall be bound thereby, any thing in the constitution or laws of any state to the contrary notwithstanding.

(3) The senators and representatives before mentioned, and the members of the several state legislatures, and all executive and judicial officers, both of the United States and of the several states, shall be bound by oath or affirmation, to support this Constitution; but no religious test shall ever be required as a qualification to any office or public trust under the United States.

ARTICLE VII
Ratifying the Constitution

The ratification of the conventions of nine states, shall be sufficient for the establishment of this Constitution between the states so ratifying the same.

Done in convention by the unanimous consent of the states present the seventeenth day of September in the year of our Lord one thousand seven hundred and eighty-seven and of the independence of the United States of America the twelfth. In witness whereof we have hereunto subscribed our names.

Amendments to the Constitution

The first ten amendments, known as the Bill of Rights, were proposed on September 25, 1789. They were ratified, or accepted, on December 15, 1791. They were adopted because some states refused to approve the Constitution unless a Bill of Rights, protecting individuals from various unjust acts of government, was added.

Amendment 1

Freedom of religion, speech, and the press;
rights of assembly and petition

Amendment 2

Right to bear arms

Amendment 3

Housing of soldiers

Amendment 4

Search and arrest warrants

Amendment 5

Rights in criminal cases

Amendment 6

Rights to a fair trial

Amendment 7

Rights in civil cases

Amendment 8

Bails, fines, and punishments

Amendment 9

Rights retained by the people

Amendment 10

Powers retained by the states and the people

Amendment 11

Lawsuits against states

Amendment 12

Election of the President and Vice President

Amendment 13

Abolition of slavery

Amendment 14

Civil rights

Amendment 15
African-American suffrage

Amendment 16
Income taxes

Amendment 17
Direct election of senators

Amendment 18
Prohibition of liquor

Amendment 19
Women's suffrage

Amendment 20
Terms of the President and Congress

Amendment 21
Repeal of prohibition

Amendment 22
Presidential term limits

Amendment 23
Suffrage in the District of Columbia

Amendment 24
Poll taxes

Amendment 25
Presidential disability and succession

Amendment 26
Suffrage for eighteen-year-olds

Amendment 27
Congressional salaries

Chapter Notes

Chapter 1

1. "2 Kids, 1 Loaded Gun, 1 Dead," *Pioneer Press*, St. Paul, Minn., November 5, 1996, p. 2A.

2. John Windrow, "Left Searching for Answers," *Star Tribune*, Minneapolis, Minn., June 30, 1996, p. 1.

3. Daniel Pedersen and Sarah Von Boven, "Tragedy in a Small Place," *Newsweek*, December 15, 1997, pp. 30–31.

4. National Safety Council, *Accident Facts* (Itasca, Ill.: National Safety Council, 1997), p. 121.

5. *Uniform Crime Reports: Crime in the United States* (Washington, D.C.: U.S. Department of Justice, Federal Bureau of Investigation, 1995), p. 18.

6. *Accident Facts*, p. 121.

7. United States Constitution, Second Amendment, December 15, 1791.

Chapter 2

1. Magna Carta (1215), Provisions 20–22, 38–40.

2. Milton Meltzer, *The Bill of Rights: How We Got It and What It Means* (New York: Thomas Y. Crowell, 1990), pp. 5, 6.

3. Geraldine Woods and Harold Woods, *The Right to Bear Arms* (New York: Franklin Watts, 1986), p. 8.

4. Ibid., pp. 8–9.

Chapter 3

1. Geraldine Woods and Harold Woods, *The Right to Bear Arms* (New York: Franklin Watts, 1986), p. 12.

2. Ibid.

3. Ibid., p. 14.

4. Alden R. Carter, *The American Revolution: War for Independence* (New York: Franklin Watts, 1992), pp. 58–59.

5. Stephen P. Halbrook, *That Every Man Be Armed: The Evolution of a Constitutional Right* (Oakland, Calif.: The Independent Institute, 1994), pp. 64–65.

6. Virginia Declaration of Rights, Article 13, June 12, 1776.

7. Declaration of Independence, July 4, 1776.

8. Bonnie L. Lukes, *The American Revolution* (San Diego, Calif.: Lucent Books, 1996), p. 86.

Chapter 4

1. James Madison, *Debates on the Adoption of the Federal Constitution in the Convention Held at Philadelphia in 1787*, ed. Jonathan Elliot (Philadelphia: J. B. Lippincott Company, 1981), p. 554.

2. Ibid., p. 538.

3. Robert A. Rutland, ed., *The Papers of James Madison*, vol. 12, p. 201, as quoted in Wilbur Ebel, *Gun Control: Threat to Liberty or Defense Against Anarchy* (Westport, Conn.: Praeger/Greenwood, 1995), p. 148.

4. United States Constitution, Second Amendment, December 15, 1791.

Chapter 5

1. Stephen Sposato in "Assault Weapons: A View From the Front Lines," hearing before the U.S. Senate Committee on the Judiciary, August. 3, 1993. U.S. Government Printing Office, Washington, D.C., serial no. J-103-2, 1994, p. 39.

2. James J. Fortis in Ibid., p. 146.

3. Keith Bea and James Saylor, "Gun Control," Congressional Research Service, Library of Congress, September 18, 1996, pp. 1, 4.

4. National Firearms Act of 1934, Public Law 73-474, 48 Stat. 1236; 26 U.S.C. 5801 et seq.

5. Federal Firearms Act of 1938, Public Law 75-785, 52 Stat. 1250.

6. Gun Control Act of 1968, Public Law 90-618, 82 Dysy. 1213; 18 U.S.C. 921 et seq.

7. Firearms Owners' Protection Act of 1986, Public Law 99-308, 100 Stat. 449; 18 U.S.C. 921 et. seq.

8. Law Enforcement Officers' Protection Act of 1986, Public Law 99-408, 100 Stat. 920; Violent Crime Control and Law Enforcement Act of 1994, Public Law 103-322, 108 Stat. 1796, sec. 110519, Armor-Piercing Ammunition Ban.

9. Undetectable Firearms Act of 1988, Public Law 100-649, 102 Stat. 3816; 18 U.S.C 922 et. seq.

10. Federal Energy Management Improvement Act of 1988, Public Law 100-615, 102 Stat. 3185; 15 U.S.C. 5001, sec. 4.

11. Gun-Free School Zones Act of 1990, Public Law 101-647, 104 Stat. 4789, sec. 1702; 18 U.S.C. 921 et. seq.

12. Brady Handgun Violence Prevention Act of 1993, Public Law 103-159, 107 Stat. 1536; 18 U.S.C. 921 et seq.

13. *Printz* v. *United States*, no. 95-1478 (1997).

14. Violent Crime Control and Law Enforcement Act of 1994, Public Law 103-322, 108 Stat. 1796.

15. Omnibus Federal Crime Law of 1996, Public Law 104.

16. "The Gun Violence Prevention Act—Brady II, Questions and Answers," Handgun Control, Inc. (Washington, D.C.: 1996).

Chapter 6

1. Stephen P. Halbrook, *That Every Man Be Armed: The Evolution of a Constitutional Right* (Oakland, Calif.: The Independent Institute, 1994), p. 156.

2. *United States* v. *Cruikshank*, 92 U.S. 542 (1875).

3. *Presser* v. *Illinois*, 116 U.S. 252 (1886).

4. *Miller* v. *Texas*, 153 U.S. 535 (1894).

5. Ibid., p. 538.

6. *United States* v. *Miller*, 307 U.S. 174 (1939).

7. Gun-Free School Zones Act of 1990, Public Law 101-647, 104 Stat. 4789, sec. 1702; 18 U.S.C. 921 et seq.

8. *United States* v. *Lopez*, 115 S. Ct. 1624 (1995).

9. *Printz* v. *United States*, no. 95-1478 (1997).

10. Ibid.

Chapter 7

1. "1997 NRA Firearms Fact Card" (Fairfax, Va.: National Rifle Association/Institute for Legislative Action, January 1997), p. 1.

2. *Oregon* v. *Owenby*, 826 P.2d 51 (Or. App. 1992).

3. *Application of Atkinson*, 291 N.W.2d 396 (Minn. 1980).

4. *Schubert* v. *DeBard*, 398 N.E.2d 1339 (Ind. 1980).

5. *Sandidge* v. *United States*, 520 A.2d 1057 (D.C. App. 1987).

6. *Kelley* v. *R.G. Industries, Inc.*, 497 A.2d 1143 (Md., 1985).

7. *State* v. *Barnhardt*, 680 P.2d 7 (Or. App. 1984).

8. *United States* v. *Oakes*, 564 F.2d 384 (1977).

9. *City of East Cleveland* v. *Scales*, 460 NE.2d 1126 (Ohio App. 1983).

10. *State* v. *Boyce*, 658 P.2d 577 (Or. App. 1983).

11. *Quilici* v. *Village of Morton Grove*, 695 F.2d 261 (Ill. 1982); *Kalodimos* v. *Village of Morton Grove*, 447 N.E.2d 849 (Ill. App. 1 Dist. 1983).

Chapter 8

1. "The Gun Violence Prevention Act of 1994: Public Health and Child Safety," hearing before the U.S. Senate Subcommittee of the Committee on the Judiciary, March 23, 1994, serial no. J-103-47, U.S. Government Printing Office, Washington D.C., 1995, p. 82.

2. Virginia Declaration of Rights, Article 13, June 12, 1776.

3. Thomas Jefferson, Proposals for the Virginia Constitution, 1776.

4. James Madison, "The Federalist Papers," no. 46 (1788).

5. "Armed Citizens and Police Officers" (Fairfax, Va.: National Rifle Association/Institute for Legal Research, 1996), p. 4.

6. Gary Kleck and Marc Gertz, "Armed Resistance to Crime: The Prevalence and Nature of Self-Defense With a Gun," *The Journal of Criminal Law and Criminology*, vol. 86, no. 1, Fall 1995, p. 150.

7. National Safety Council, *Accident Facts* (Itasca, Ill.: National Safety Council, 1997), p. 43.

8. Ibid., p. 32.

9. Ibid., p. 43.

10. "Firearms Registration: New York City's Lesson," fact sheet, National Rifle Association (Fairfax, Va.: 1996), p. 1.

11. Administrative Code and Charter of the City of New York, sec. 10-303.1.

12. Florida Statutes, sec. 790.06.

13. "The Right to Carry Firearms," fact sheet, National Rifle Association/Institute for Legal Research (Fairfax, Va.: May 1996), p. 1.

14. "Ten Myths About Gun Control," fact sheet, National Rifle Association/Institute for Legal Research (Fairfax, Va.: March 1996), p. 13.

15. "Second Amendment to the U.S. Constitution," fact sheet, National Rifle Association/Institute for Legal Research (Fairfax, Va.: 1995), p. 3.

16. Kennesaw, Georgia, Ordinance, sec. 8-10, March 15, 1982.

17. "Handgun Bans: A History of Failure," fact sheet, National Rifle Association/Institute for Legal Research (Fairfax, Va.: 1996), p. 2.

18. "Ten Myths About Gun Control," pp. 1, 2.

19. Kleck and Gertz, p. 150.

20. "Armed Citizens and Police Officers," p. 1.

21. "Correcting the Failure of America's Criminal Justice System," fact sheet, CrimeStrike, National Rifle Association (Fairfax, Va.: 1996), p. 1.

22. National Rifle Association Bylaws, Article II.

23. "Eddie Eagle Educator Notes," fact sheet, National Rifle Association (Fairfax, Va.: 1996), p. 2.

24. "Gun Control," CRS Issue Brief, Library of Congress, September 18, 1996, p. 2.

25. "Gun Safety Rules: Three Fundamental Rules for Safe Gun Handling," fact sheet, National Rifle Association (Fairfax, Va.: 1995), p. 1.

Chapter 9

1. Tom Vandenberk, "Establishing Solutions for Problems of Gun Violence," hearing before the U.S. Senate Committee on the Judiciary, January 31, 1994, serial no. J-103-38, U.S. Government Printing Office, Washington, D.C., 1995, pp. 18–19.

2. National Safety Council, *Accident Facts* (Itasca, Ill.: National Safety Council, 1997), p. 121.

3. Ibid., p. 10.

4. *United States v. Miller*, 307 U.S. 174 (1939).

5. "The Second Amendment: Myth & Meaning," pamphlet (Washington, D.C.: Center to Prevent Handgun Violence, no date), pp. 2–3.

6. Warren E. Burger, "The Right to Bear Arms," *Parade*, January 14, 1990, pp. 4–6.

7. *Accident Facts 1997 Edition*, p. 121.

8. Ibid.

9. "Firearms & Youth Suicide," fact sheet (Washington, D.C.: Center to Prevent Handgun Violence, April 1996), quoting F. L. Annest, *Journal of the American Medical Association*, 1995.

10. Ibid., quoting National Center for Health Statistics, 1991.

11. Ibid., quoting Centers for Disease Control, 1995.

12. Ibid., quoting University of Minnesota Medical School, University of Minnesota Clinic and Hospital.

13. *Accident Facts 1997 Edition*, p. 121.

14. J. Alex Haller, Jr., in "Children and Gun Violence," hearing before the U.S. Senate Committee on the Judiciary, June 9, 1993, and September 13, 1993, hearing, serial no. J-103-18, U.S. Government Printing Office, Washington, D.C., 1994, p. 55.

15. Ibid.

16. Ibid.

17. M. Joycelyn Elders, in "The Gun Violence Prevention Act of 1994: Public Health and Child Safety," hearing before the U.S. Senate Subcommittee of the Committee on the Judiciary, March 23, 1994, serial No. J-103-47, U.S. Government Printing Office, Washington, D.C., 1995, pp. 6–7.

18. Kellermann, in Ibid., p. 61.

19. "Do Guns Make Us Safe?" fact sheet (Washington, D.C.: Center to Prevent Handgun Violence, April 1996), quoting D. McCowall, *American Journal of Public Health*, 1994.

20. Elders in "The Gun Violence Prevention Act of 1994," p. 6.

21. "Guns in our Nation's Schools," fact sheet (Washington, D.C.: Center to Prevent Handgun Violence, April 1996), quoting C. Ginsberg, *Journal of School Health*, 1993.

22. Ibid., quoting J. F. Sheley, *Public Health Reports*, 1995.

23. Ibid., quoting L H Research, Inc., 1993.

24. Ibid., quoting of Virginia State Department of Education, 1991–92 school year.

25. Senator Paul Simon in "Establishing Solutions for Problems of Gun Violence," p. 14.

26. Ibid.

27. "Economic Costs of Gun Violence," fact sheet (Washington, D.C.: Center to Prevent Handgun Violence, April 1996), quoting K.W. Kizer, *Journal of the American Medical Association*, 1995.

28. Ibid., quoting Centers for Disease Control, 1990.

29. Joseph L. Wright, in "The Gun Violence Prevention Act of 1994," p. 29.

30. *Printz* v. *United States*, Supreme Court Opinions, June 27, 1997, no. 95-1478.

31. "Gun Laws Work," fact sheet (Washington, D.C.: Center to Prevent Handgun Violence, April 1996), quoting from BATF Brady Law First Anniversary Survey.

32. Ibid., p. 1.

33. Ibid., p. 2.

34. "A Report for Congress: Firearms Regulation: Comparative Overviews of Selected Foreign Nations," Law Library staff of the Law Library of Congress, August 1994.

35. "The Dunblane Effect," *Newsweek*, October 28, 1996, p. 46.

36. "Gun Laws Work," pp. 2–3.

37. Dewey R. Stokes, in "Children and Gun Violence," pp. 21–22.

38. "Firearms & Youth Suicide," fact sheet (Washington, D.C.: Center to Prevent Handgun Violence, April 1996), quoting Brent, *General Psychiatry*, 1988.

39. "Do Guns Make Us Safe?" quoting A. Kellermann, *New England Journal of Medicine*, 1993.

Chapter 10

1. M. Joycelyn Elders, in "The Gun Violence Prevention Act of 1994: Public Health and Child Safety," hearing before the U.S. Senate Subcommittee of the Committee on the Judiciary, March 23, 1994, serial no. J-103-47, U.S. Government Printing Office, Washington, D.C., 1995, p. 7.

2. Sarah Brady, in "Children and Gun Violence," hearing before the U.S. Senate Committee on the Judiciary, June 9, 1993, and September 13, 1993, serial no. J-103-18, U.S. Government Printing Office, Washington, D.C., 1994, p. 159.

3. Joseph L. Wright, in "The Gun Violence Prevention Act of 1994," p. 29.

4. "STAR (Straight Talk About Risks), a Pre-K–12th Grade Curriculum for Preventing Gun Violence" (Washington, D.C.: Center to Prevent Handgun Violence, no date).

5. "STOP (Steps to Prevent Firearm Injury)," American Academy of Pediatrics and Center to Prevent Handgun Violence, 1996, quoting National Center for Health Statistics.

6. Ibid., quoting A. L. Kellermann, *New England Journal of Medicine*, 1992, 1993.

7. Ibid., quoting *Los Angeles Times* poll, January 1994.

8. Author interview with Jennifer Fling, Hennepin County Attorneys Office, Minneapolis, Minn., November 19, 1996.

9. Dewey R. Stokes, in "Children and Gun Violence," p. 24.

Chapter 11

1. Ruben Rosario, "Shoes for a Silent March," *Pioneer Press*, St. Paul, Minn., September 18, 1996, p. 1.

Glossary

ammunition—Bullets and shells belonging to a gun.

automatic weapon—A firearm that allows a person to shoot a series of bullets in rapid succession by holding down the trigger.

Bill of Rights—The first ten amendments to the United States Constitution, which guarantee certain freedoms. They were approved December 15, 1791.

bulletproof vest—A protective article of clothing that law-enforcement officers wear on the upper part of the body as protection from bullets.

concealed weapon—A firearm hidden from plain view. A permit is required in many states to carry a concealed weapon.

Constitutional Convention—Meeting at which representatives of the states met in Philadelphia in the summer of 1787 to create a new government for the United States.

felony—A very serious crime punishable by fine and imprisonment for at least one year. Murder, burglary, and rape are all felonies.

gun control—Efforts to control the purchase, manufacture, and sale of firearms.

handgun—A small weapon made to fire a small bullet and to be held in one hand. It has a short barrel.

magazine—A detachable clip or box where cartridges of bullets are held until they are fed into the firing chamber of a gun for discharge.

misdemeanor—A crime less serious than a felony, punishable by a smaller fine and jail time of less than one year.

rifle—A long-barreled gun in which a single bullet is fired through a rifle bore (inside of the barrel through which the bullet travels) by a single pull of the trigger.

shotgun—A firearm in which a single shell (larger than a bullet) containing pellets is fired through a smooth bore (the inside of the barrel through which the shell travels) by a single pull of the trigger.

state right—A right that the states maintain control over. Some argue that the right to control firearms is a state right.

unconstitutional law—A law that the Supreme Court has declared in violation of either the United States Constitution or a state constitution.

United States Congress—The Senate and the House of Representatives, responsible for making laws.

United States Constitution—Ratified in 1788, it became the basic law forming the United States government as it is today. It consists of seven articles and twenty-seven amendments.

United States Supreme Court—The highest court in the land; its nine Justices have the final say over whether or not a law is constitutional.

waiting period—The time between registering to purchase a gun and actually taking it home.

Further Reading

The United States Government and the Constitution

Citizenship in the Nation. Irving, Tex.: Boy Scouts of America, 1993.

Judson, Karen. *The Constitution of the United States.* Springfield, N.J.: Enslow Publishers Inc., 1996.

The Bill of Rights

Mork, Linda R. *The Bill of Rights: A User's Guide.* Second ed. Close Up Foundation, 1995.

Gun Control

Bosch, Carl. *Schools Under Siege: Guns, Gangs, and Hidden Dangers.* Springfield, N.J.: Enslow Publishers, Inc., 1997.

Cox, Vic. *Guns, Violence, and Teens.* Springfield, N.J.: Enslow Publishers, Inc., 1997.

Jacobs, Nancy R., Norma Jones, and Mark A. Siegel. *Gun Control: An American Issue.* Wylie, Tex.: Information Plus, 1994.

Kruschke, Earl R. *Gun Control: A Reference Handbook.* Santa Barbara, Calif.: ABC-CLIO, Inc., 1995.

Murray, James M. *50 Things You Can Do About Guns.* San Francisco: Robert D. Reed Publishers, 1994.

Roleff, Tamara L., ed. *Gun Control: Opposing Viewpoints.* San Diego, Calif.: Greenhaven Press, Inc., 1997.

Woods, Geraldine, and Harold Woods. *The Right to Bear Arms.* New York: Franklin Watts, 1986.

Legal Internet Site

http://court.it-services.nwu.edu/oyez/cases/search.pl

Index